CALIFORNIA
& THE GOLDEN WEST

Welcome to

California and the Golden West

Carole Chester

Collins
Glasgow and London

For Graham

Cover photographs

Van Phillips
(top; Mason Street, San Francisco, mid left; Golden Gate Bridge, San Francisco,
mid right; Bright Angel Trail, Grand Canyon, bottom left; Sunset Blvd, Los Angeles
bottom right; entrance, Caesar's Palace, Las Vegas)

Photographs

All by Van Phillips except:
pp 44 right, 73, 75 (Featurepix); 72, 74 left (J. Allan Cash); 74 right (ZEFA)

Regional maps

Mike Shand, Kažia L. Kram, Iain Gerard

Town plans

M. & R. Piggott

Illustration

pp 6–7 Peter Joyce

First published 1983
Copyright © text: Carole Chester
Copyright © maps: Wm. Collins Sons & Co. Ltd
Published by William Collins Sons and Company Limited
Printed in Great Britain

ISBN 0 00 447326 4

HOW TO USE THIS BOOK

The contents page of this book shows how the area is divided up into tourist regions.
The book is in two sections; general information and gazetteer.
In the gazetteer each tourist region is introduced and
has a regional map (detail below left).
There are also plans of the main cities (detail below right).
All the cities and towns in the gazetteer are shown on the regional maps.
Places to visit and leisure facilities available in each
region and city are indicated by symbols. Main highways,
railroads and airports are shown on the maps and plans.

Regional Maps

▣	Museum/gallery	🐘	Zoo/safari park
✝	Religious building	ϻ	Ancient monument
✈	Main airport	♣	Park
✈	Other airport	⚕	Spa
▥	Castle	⛏	Caves/mines
▲	Climbing	⬧	Walking/hiking
⊞	Interesting building	🦌	Wild life reserve
⚓	Boating/sailing	⚑	Water sports
❊	Gardens	⚑	Canoeing
⊛	Amusement park	⚑	Scuba diving
⛷	Skiing/winter sports		

1 : 3 000 000

```
0        25              50 miles
0              50            100 kms
```

══════	four lane divided highway
══════	principal highway
──────	railroad

Town Plans

Museum/gallery	▣
Religious building	✝
Interesting building	⊞
Theatre	☻
Library	▥
City hall	✄
Post office	✉
Information	ℹ
Police	POL
Park	♣
Garden	❊
Station	●
Bus depot	▭
Parking lot	Ⓟ
Hospital	⊕

feet	meters
9000	2743
6000	1829
3000	914
1500	457
600	183
0 Land Dep.	0 Land Dep.

Every effort has been made to give you an up-to-date text but changes are constantly occurring and we will be grateful for any information about changes you may notice while travelling.

CONTENTS

3

CALIFORNIA

During the 16th century only Indian tribes occupied what we now know as California. While many explorers sighted it, a number of them, seeing only the lower peninsula, thought they had come across another island, and very few actually landed. Although they were not about to pass up any treasure they could pick up along the way, most of those early explorers, like Columbus and Cabrillo, were seeking shorter trade routes to the East Indies.

In the early 1540s, Spain was rich and powerful; Spanish explorers extended their country's knowledge of northern Pacific waters; and Spain got to California first. The name California is from a Spanish story which told of an island inhabited by black Amazons which lay 'at the right hand of The Indies..very close to that part of the Terrestrial Paradise'. The name was first used for the Pacific coastline in the early 1530s.

Who really discovered what and when remains somewhat unclear but the major credit for the discovery of California can essentially be given to Cabrillo, who although Portuguese by birth, was with Cortez when he conquered Mexico. It was Cabrillo who founded, in 1542, what was later to become San Diego. (Sir Francis Drake, by the way, didn't get around to California until 1579 when he called the coast New Albion.)

So when Juan Rodriguez Cabrillo sailed into that lower Californian bay (so close to Mexico itself), naming the place San Miguel (San Diego), it became 'the birthplace of California'. It wasn't, however, until 60 years later that the Spanish explorer, Sebastian Vizcaino, renamed the harbor San Diego, during a famous voyage in which he charted the coast and discovered the bay of Monterey.

Over 150 years had passed before Spain decided to send soldiers and priests into this new area to establish communities and convert the Indians to Christianity, which is how California's missions came into being. In fact, it wasn't until 1769 that Father Junipero Serra set up the first of what was to become a chain of 21 missions – Mission San Diego de Alcala.

In the interim, different other bits of California were intermittently 'discovered'. Drake happened upon one of the bays along the upper California coast while on his way back to England, and promptly claimed it for the British crown. Francisco Gali found the Cape Mendocino area in 1584 and Rodriguez de Carmenho reached another point above Point Reyes in 1595. Vizcaino named Catalina Island, Santa Barbara, Monterey, and Carmel, among other places.

The main reason for Spain's decision to do something about establishing real settlements was to combat the potential danger from the British who by 1763 were sharing a common frontier with the Spanish in the Mississippi valley. Not to mention a different potential danger from the Russians who at that same time were probing further into the northern Pacific in search of furs.

The 1769 arrivées in San Diego brought vegetable and flower seeds as well as cattle with them. The cattle were to give California much of its wealth in future years. During this time, Serra's time, the plan was to set up five missions in upper California. These were to be the state's first system of government and education and it was due to their farms that it was learnt that such products as dates and citrus fruits could flourish well in California. In fact, in his lifetime, Serra founded nine of the 21 missions and the rest were established by Father Fermin Francisco de Lasuén.

Spain aimed at a 30-mile (48km) separation (or one day's horseback ride) between the missions and built presidios and pueblos to defend and support them. Certainly they mushroomed with relative speed. After San Diego, the second mission was sited at Monterey – San Carlos Borromeo – in 1770, although later it was moved to Carmel which had better wood and water. San Antonio de Padua was founded in 1771 and later that year, San Gabriel Arcángel (a mission which continues to be famous for its bells and museum containing early California treasures). The success of these early struggling missions was undoubtedly helped by the presence (in 1771) of a strong Spanish viceroy in Mexico – Antonio Bucareli.

The 'Prince of Missions' – San Luis Obispo de Tolosa – was established in 1772 but it took four more years before

San Francisco de Asis, which became known as Mission Dolores for its proximity to Dolores Creek, was founded in 1776. 'Jewel of the Missions' – San Juan Capistrano dates from the same year. In 1777, Santa Clara, which was to suffer a great deal from natural elements, was founded and in 1782, San Buenaventura. 'Queen of the Missions' – Santa Barbara (1786) at one time served as a beacon for ships. La Purisima Concepción was a mission founded in 1787 and Santa Cruz in 1791, followed by Nuestra Señora de la Soledad.

California's earliest civic pueblo was San José de Guadalupe (1797). Three other missions were founded in that year: San Juan Bautista, San Miguel Arcángel and San Fernando Rey de España. San Luis Rey de Francia came about in 1798 and 'Mission of the Passes' – Santa Inés, in 1804. San Rafael Arcángel (1817) was originally designed as a health retreat for padres and the last before the collapse of the system was San Francisco Solano in 1823.

Despite what one may think to the contrary, during the mission era there were relatively few troubles with the indians and only an event like the Yuma Massacre (when the Yuma Indians attacked two missions) really stands out. In such cases it was unfair treatment by the Spanish which provoked violence.

Indeed it was not the Indians who posed any real threat to Spanish settlers, but the Russian and American traders who began to turn up in the early 1800s. The Russians had already established settlements in Alaska and were moving into San Francisco for trading purposes around 1806, setting up Fort Ross in 1812. American traders made their debut around 1796 and were eventually the cause of the breakdown of Spanish restrictions on the area.

In 1822, Spanish authority was transferred to Mexico which proceeded to make San Diego its Californian capital. Having won its independence from Spain, Mexico began to issue a number of land grants so that by 1824, big cattle ranches were replacing the mission system. Cattle were important to California from the very earliest mission, but now that individuals could own several ranchos and ranching proved profitable, a number of family fortunes were made. Ranch owners became known as the 'Silver Dons' for the silver adornments they wore on their clothes and saddles. Lack of fences around the ranchos led to the rodeo – the rounding up and branding of animals to distinguish one owner's cattle from another's.

The 1840s made a considerable impact on California. It was the decade when America took over, and it was the decade for gold! Once the Russians moved out in 1842, it was the increased stream of American traders who became Mexico's threat. Many were trappers. Many came by wagon train. Some, like Kit Carson, were to earn legendary names; others achieved a different king of glory. Johann Sutter, for example, planned a fort on the site of what was to become Sacramento. He named his fort New Helvetica for his native country.

The first time that an American flag was raised in California was 1846 when US forces defeated the Mexicans at the Battle of San Pascual and General Frémont took San Diego. He also moved into Los Angeles (at that time little more than a hamlet), but his new garrison couldn't hold out and it was only reclaimed for the US by Stockton and General Stephen Kearny in the following year. San Francisco, at this time, was an even tinier hamlet which only began to expand with the arrival of a couple of hundred Mormons and, subsequently, gold prospectors.

The discovery of gold left an indelible mark on Californian history. Although Indians had discovered a little of the precious metal near Los Angeles in 1841 and, later, there were various other findings, it was James Wilson Marshall's 1848 find around Sutter's fort that attracted everyone's attention. Gold fever started and there was a rush to the Sierra.

A population of 26,000 (non-Indians) in California at the beginning of 1849 suddenly swelled to 100,000 by the end of the same year. Gold was very definitely the reason for San Francisco's boom and its own population increased from 1000 in 1848 to 25,000 by 1850. New towns literally sprang up in mining areas and prices of basic goods were highly inflated. The peak year for gold was 1852 and when it declined, many miners returned to the cities leaving ghost towns behind them.

Miners who stayed turned to banking, farming, and fishing.

The 1850s were a period of unrest for California. Large numbers of immigrants, especially Chinese, plus lack of enough women were factors leading to social unrest. Hence, the instigation of the Vigilantes. Whether or not they were much more than a lynch mob is a moot point. The Vigilantes Committee was originally formed in San Francisco to ensure law and order in that city since the city government itself showed no signs of doing anything about the crime, vice, and corruption practiced openly. Unfortunately, in their pursuance of law and order, they over-reacted rashly in some cases, often persecuting foreigners needlessly. However, they did help to overcome lawlessness and even after their dissolution, San Francisco remained reasonably well governed for several years.

Transportation was a key element in the growth of the West, starting with the stage coach, used first for miners and bullion and then for mail. The first stage ran in 1849 but it wasn't until 1860 that San Francisco became the terminus of the Pony Express. This system, which utilized relays of horses between various points, was introduced because it allowed mail to reach its destination faster than by stage. One of the most famous Pony Express riders was a man by the name of 'Buffalo Bill' Cody. The system worked well for 16 months until a transcontinental telegraph line was completed in 1861.

Of the staging companies, Wells Fargo is probably the best known and best operated. It often carried gold – and it was often robbed. The Western outlaw has become another legend in this connection. Thanks to gold, an early banking system was developed, starting with a shack at a mining camp and progressing to a much better organized system. San Francisco could boast 19 banks in 1855 and although there was a banking depression following the dwindling of gold sources, by the 1860s Los Angeles was a leading banking center catering to rich farmers and ranchers.

Governmental changes caused many arguments over land title, which initiated the need for insurance companies, but in the meantime disputed land titles managed to bankrupt some of the ranchers. Indeed, the 1860s saw the break up of the enormous ranchos. Land squabbles were one reason – natural bad conditions were another. Property taxes were not in favor of the ranchers either. There is, of course, a good side to everything – because of the breakup of the ranchos, real estate development could start.

The Civil War meant relatively little to California, so that while the starting of a northern railroad was postponed, a bill was passed in Congress to allow construction to begin on a Pacific railway in 1862. America's first transcontinental rail system was not finished until 1869.

Two phrases long remembered by Californians for this association with the spread of fame and fortune, are 'The Comstock Lode' and 'The Big Four'. The former was discovered by H.T. Comstock and was rich deposits of gold and silver in western Nevada. This mineral wealth enabled men like Sutro, Mackay, Flood, and Fair to become rich. Sutro became a mayor of San Francisco and donated a library. Mackay loaned money for an international cable and telegraph system. And one of the things Fair did was create what eventually became the Fairmont Hotel.

'The Big Four' refers to the men who made their fortunes from the railroad. It was Leland Stanford, Collis Huntington and Mark Hopkins who founded the Central Pacific Railroad and who were later joined by Charles Crocker. All were California merchants, all ambitious. When the Central Pacific was completed in 1869, 'The Big Four' turned their energies to the San Francisco Bay region, the central valley, and a coastal route to southern California from Oregon. The railway brought 'new Californians' – Chinese and Irish immigrants – as workers. It also brought new towns like Fresno and Bakersfield and did a great deal to strengthen California's agricultural industry.

One has to credit the Spanish with the introduction of the crops for which California is still famous even today. The citrus fruits, olives, and walnuts were first grown, after all, in those mission gardens. From these small beginnings a great industry developed. By 1872 Los Angeles county alone had 35,000 orange trees and from there orange growing spread through the neighboring counties. Such was the expansion that fruit growers formed a marketing organization in 1893 which two years later, was to result in the founding of the Southern Fruit Growers' Exchange.

Another small beginning which has become a great industry centered on the grape! The first grape cuttings were planted in San Diego, then others were introduced at the missions of San Gabriel, Santa Barbara, and San Luis Obispo. It was German immigrants, not surprisingly, who aided this industry's development by forming the Los Angeles Vineyard Society in 1857. They bought land to the east of Los Angeles and gave it the name of Anaheim. Hungarians and French planters also lent their expertise in other areas during the 1850s so that by 1879, 150,000 acres of land had been planted with vines.

The growth of such agricultural developments plus the ever competitive railroads boosted the immigrant population even more and there were plenty of Californian towns which were in their early days almost totally immigrant communities. But by 1870, 'pioneer California' had more or less disappeared and the West's new inhabitants became more interested in culture. San Francisco, especially, became a center for the arts and suddenly writers and poets were two a penny.

Education took on a new importance. Public schools erupted everywhere; colleges were founded; and compulsory schooling was introduced in 1874. And it was in the late 1800s that San Francisco earned the reputation it retains today – for hotels and restaurants of the finest quality.

An early 19th century event that had a memorable effect was San Francisco's 1906 earthquake and fire. The earthquake, which happened along the San Andreas Fault which runs from Salinas in the south to Cape Mendocino in the north, caused even brick buildings to collapse. Short-circuited electrical wires which fell into the city streets started immediate fires which spread and raged for three days before burning themselves out. Nob Hill and Chinatown, among other sectors, were left in ruins and the total property loss and damage amounted to an astronomical figure. While in many ways this was a setback, it created employment for many in the building and allied industries and gave an incentive for city modernization. For instance, it was at this time that a cable car system was planned as part of the rebuilding program.

In Los Angeles at this time people were thinking about building a new harbor. After some wrangling, it was built at San Pedro, not Santa Monica. By 1914, Los Angeles was not only a great American harbor city, but recognized throughout the world as such.

Though the rest of the world was at war, California was progressing. And the Californians showed it in the Panama-Pacific Exposition in 1915 held in San Francisco. Another was held during that same year in San Diego. Both San Francisco and Los Angeles expanded with the aid of improved transportation systems. The Key Route Electric Railway was developed to serve San Francisco's East Bay area and the Pacific Electric in Los Angeles grew into a network that operated 900 cars over 1100 miles of track.

They might have been far away from all the fighting, but World War I stimulated California's food processing industries as well as cotton production. The demand was also strong for fresh meats, vegetables, and grain. After the war a housing boom created yet more new towns like San Clemente and Palm Springs.

A new industry for California was oil. The earliest well was drilled in 1861 in Humboldt County and the first known gusher was found in the vicinity of Ojai. The oil business didn't become successful until the 1890s while the greatest oil discoveries happened in the 1920s in the San Joaquin Valley and in the hills. Greatest strikes of all were at Huntington Beach, Santa Fe Springs and Signal Hill. It was the beginning for what are today oil company giants.

The car became a status symbol. It arrived more slowly in the West than the East, mainly because until 1910, there were many country lanes and only in the next 20 years were they transformed into two-laned concrete roads. Later four-laned blacktop highways appeared and by the 1940s, even larger freeways. Accessibility meant towns found themselves to be holiday centers, including the once-feared Death Valley, now suddenly a winter tourist attraction.

Freeway traffic, Los Angeles

Because of the car, Los Angeles' trolley system was put out of action and some railways were forced to close down. It did so well, it remained a stable industry despite the 1930-37 depression years. The 1920s and 1930s also increased banking business in the West, with the largest – Bank of America – emerging from the original Bank of Italy.

One can also say that during these years, both Los Angeles and San Francisco truly became metropolitan cities. For Los Angeles: a civic center, a government building complex, a Union passenger railroad terminal, a metropolitan water system and the foundations of the aviation industry. For San Francisco: improvements to Golden Gate Park, the building of the Bay bridges, and more artistic achievements.

The Depression drove more newcomers to the West – this time from the Mid-West Dust Bowl areas. Migrant 'Okies' and 'Arkies' arrived without work and without a homestead. Their hardships were recorded in songs by Woody Guthrie and in novels by John Steinbeck. They were not the only ones to cause problems; Mexicans flocked across the border seeking jobs, competing fiercely with the Filipinos for low paid work. Some of the migrants who arrived in southern California during the first part of the 20th century, brought strange ideas with them and started up cults and movements which would not have been accepted elsewhere in America.

In the early 20th century, Hollywood blossomed. Hollywood 'village' had played host to the film industry during World War I when in Europe the industry came to a temporary stop. In the 1920s, Hollywood became *the* film centre for the world, a place almost of make-believe where money was spent so incredibly fast and in such huge amounts, it was like Monopoly money. One epic picture followed another and men who were originally tradesmen became powerful and wealthy. Lewis Selznick, for example, had been in the jewelry business, Sam Goldwyn was a glove salesman; and Louis Mayer had been a rag collector!

During the 1930s, there had been gradual expansion of the West Coast shipyards and dry docks, but the unexpected attack on Pearl Harbor meant many more ships had to be built in a hurry, along with aircraft factories. California was already ahead in the aviation industry – Donald Douglas's design team had been responsible for Charles Lindbergh's *Spirit of St Louis*. A variety of aircraft were constructed in southern California in World War II, making an essential contribution to the American war effort. After the war was over, aircraft companies went into radar equipment, missiles, and passenger jets.

At the end of the war, San Francisco was chosen as the site for the signing of the United Nations Charter in which 46 nations pledged to form a permanent buffer against world aggression.

Post-war changes saw the diversification of manufacturing. Major industries moved into secondary cities such as Oakland and Fresno. A new range of products, like sportswear, was being made available for a greater range of people.

New highways were built and housing development started up again. Only this time, it was apartment blocks of the high-rise variety.

In the 1960s, there were riots throughout America. It was also the decade of the hippies, a time when the run-down area of Haight-Ashbury (in San Francisco) came into international focus.

Since then, California has continued to grow. There is still a multitude of orange trees (though not as many as in earlier eras); fads and fancies are still 'born' in the West; theme parks and man-made amusements are constantly created and expanded. Descendants of those first pioneers have become well and truly entrenched as native Californians.

PAPERWORK

UK citizens require a valid passport – not the temporary visitors' kind. Passport application forms are available from any post office or the Passport Office, Clive House, 70–78 Petty France, London, SW1; India Buildings, Water St, Liverpool 2; Olympia House, Upper Dock St, Newport, Gwent; 55 Westfield St, Peterborough and 1st floor, Empire House, 2 West Nile St, Glasgow. The application must be accompanied by two passport-sized photos and (for first time applicant) a birth certificate. Current cost is £11.

At the time of writing, a visa is also required (although this may change some time in 1982). Visas are issued free and application forms are available from the US Embassy, 24 Grosvenor Square, London, W1 (01 499 9000); Visa Branch, 5 Upper Grosvenor St, London, W1 (01 499 3443); and the US Consulate at 3 Regent Terrace, Edinburgh 6 (031 556 8315). Visa applications should be accompanied by a passport-sized photo.

No innoculations or vaccinations are necessary unless you are arriving from an infected area. You may be asked for evidence that you are leaving the US e.g. a return air ticket.

CURRENCY

The American monetary unit is the dollar ($) which is divided into 100 cents (¢). Coins are issued in 1-, 5-, 10-, and 25-cent denominations. A five-cent piece is known as a 'nickel'; a 10-cent piece as a 'dime', and a 25-cent piece as a 'quarter'. Exact change is needed for telephones and often for city transportation. Occasionally, you will come across a half dollar (50¢) in coin form.

In note form, the dollar is issued in 1, 2, 5, 10, 20, 50, and 100 denominations. It is wiser to carry notes in smaller amounts especially for paying taxis as obtaining large amounts of change out of $50 and $100 notes is difficult.

There is no limit on how much foreign currency is taken in or out of America. It may be changed at any bank with exchange facilities (all the major ones) during normal banking hours; anywhere you see 'Exchange'; and at all top hotels. Dollar travellers' cheques may be purchased in advance of departure.

HOW TO GET THERE

By Air

From the UK Los Angeles and San Francisco are both international gateway cities served by European carriers and American transatlantic carriers ex-UK. Major airlines offering direct service are: British Airways, Pan Am, and TWA, all on a scheduled basis. Prices are highly variable dependent upon season, category of service, and type of booking arrangement.

The three standard fare structures are: First Class, Economy and Excursion (which has a minimum and maximum period of stay – 14–21 days or 22–45 days). These days many of the carriers have added a 'Business Class' fare (which goes by a variety of other names), featuring a little more luxury than Economy but a little less than First.

An APEX (advance purchase excursion) fare is one of the cheapest ways to guarantee a seat on a specific flight, but the ticket must be bought and paid for at least 21 days in advance and you will be subject to a cancellation fee. When standby and budget fares are available, they will be cheaper but there are restrictions. Standby seat allocations are only made on the departure day so there is no security of getting on. Budget travellers can only specify the week they wish to travel but the airline decides on day and time of flight you get to use.

Charter flights (ABCs) are only sold

through travel agents or tour operators like Jetsave. They must be purchased at least 21 days in advance, have a minimum stay requirement and flight timings cannot be altered, once made. Inclusive American package holidays often make use of charter flights although they may equally take advantage of regular scheduled air services.

Major airlines operating a London-Los Angeles route are: British Airways, Pan Am, TWA. Operating a London-San Francisco route: British Airways, TWA. Operating London–San Diego: TWA. Air Canada services America's West Coast from Canada and major airlines operating from America's East Coast to Western gateways, are: Eastern Airlines, American, TWA, United, Pan Am, and World Airwways.

By Sea
There are no direct crossings from Southampton to the West Coast, but some cruises, e.g. P&O, do visit Los Angeles and San Francisco. Passenger-carrying cargo ships such as Johnson Lines also sometimes visit these ports.

By Car
Travelling by car is, not surprisingly, the best way to see most of The Golden West and economical for families. America is geared to automobile travel and highway and freeway facilities are some of the world's finest. Car rental is readily available. When not included in a fly/drive package, cars may be rented on the spot at airports from major firms like Hertz and Avis. In the US, categories of car are usually 'economy', 'compact', and 'standard'. ('Economy' size is equivalent to standard European size).

Each car rental firm features its own packages as well as two standard rates: per day/per mile charge or a per day/unlimited mileage. The second of these is the more viable for anyone planning to tour a great deal. Most firms require the driver to be at least 21 (in some cases older) and to have a valid driver's license – a UK license is valid for use up to a year. Local rental firms may be cheaper but check whether pickup and return points can be different – a necessity if you are travelling inter-city or inter-state. Avis, Budget, and Hertz all have UK offices and among others represented in the UK are Dollars-A-Day Rent-A-Car and National.

The American Automobile Association and the British AA have a reciprocal arrangement for breakdown and other services. British AA card members should ensure their card is stamped before leaving for the US. RAC members will need to take out its Cordon Bleu service for covering breakdowns etc.

By Plane
Shuttle flights e.g.: between San Francisco and Los Angeles, can be very reasonable and arranged once in the US. The London offices of American carriers are: American Airlines, Braniff, Continental, Delta, Eastern, Hughes Airwest, National/Pan Am, Northwest Orient, TWA, United and Western. Sightseeing excursions by air of the Grand Canyon are best arranged from Las Vegas.

By Train
If plans call for a great deal of train travel within the US, a USA Rail Pass is worth buying before departing from the UK. It entitles the holder to unlimited travel for specific durations at discounted prices. Thomas Cook is the British agent for Amtrak.

By Bus
The two major coach companies – Greyhound and Continental Trailways (both with UK offices) feature special passes for overseas visitors if purchased outside the continental US. (They can also be obtained from travel agents.) In both cases, passes allow unlimited travel on the companies' routes for specified number of days for a flat rate. Both firms promote their own packages within the US including accommodations. Often bus travel will prove the most economical way of reaching points of interest e.g.: Los Angeles – Disneyland.

Getting Around Los Angeles
The bus system in Greater Los Angeles has greatly improved in the last few years. Visitors (out of state or foreign) may purchase cheap go-as-you-please tickets for specified numbers of days. They are given a pack that includes maps, route listings, timetables, and other general information. Some of the freeway lanes are now marked 'Busways' to be used exclusively by RTD. The scheme also covers downtown mini buses, airport terminal shuttles, and express buses from airport to city. There is also frequent express bus service to such places as Universal Studios and Long Beach.

Getting Around San Francisco
The Metropolitan area is served by an efficient bus system at low cost. Detailed route information can be obtained at the Municipal Transit office at 949 Presidio

Ave. Included in this system are four streetcar lines which operate on Market St and branch off to other parts of the city.

There are only three remaining cable car routes but they're still the best way of getting over the city's hills. The most popular with tourists is No. 60 which can be picked up at Powell and Market Sts, and travels over Nob and Russian Hills.

BART (Bay Area Rapid Transport) is the quick way to reach outlying places

such as Oakland, Richmond, Daly City, and Fremont. This high-speed rapid-transit rail system is easy to use and shows routes and fares at each station.

Getting Around Las Vegas

As cities go, Las Vegas is not large – it isn't far from downtown to the Strip. However, the Las Vegas Transit System does cover both areas by bus.

Cable car, San Francisco

Bay Area Rapid Transport

ACCOMMODATION

The chain hotel was developed in America to provide standardized comfort and service. They do just that and the level of accommodations in the USA is probably higher than anywhere else in the world. Most of the chain hotel companies have a toll-free number within America to call for reservations and the big names have their own offices (or hotel representation) in the UK and Europe.

At the top end of the scale, there are Hyatts and Hiltons which are luxurious and feature every possible amenity, but naturally they are quite pricey. Then there is the motel. Some of these, too, can be quite plush and offer plenty of facilities. (Chain names to look out for include Best Western and TraveLodge.) But others are more than suitable for the budget-minded, mostly located on the fringes of the large cities and along the highways linking places of interest. Large chain hotels and motels usually offer a variety of rate structures – e.g.: weekend packages, business traveller discounts.

Las Vegas hotels need a special mention because the large ones (like Caesar's Palace) house casinoes. In fact, in many cases one has to walk through a forest of fruit machines to reach the front desk! Even the lower-priced motels without the fully fledged casino, have installed fruit machines to encourage you to lose your money.

Some of America's most famous hotels are located in the Golden West – es-

tablishments of historical importance or places which have acquired a reputation as the places for 'seeing' the famous or for 'being seen in'. Among the most prominent in San Francisco are: *Stanford Court*, 905 California St, which was built on the site of Leland Stanford's mansion, with true Nob Hill elegance. Service and decor is far more Europeanized than most hotels. The drive-in courtyard is covered by a Tiffany-style glass dome and one of the plus factors warranting high room rates, are the miniature TVs in the bathrooms. The *Mark Hopkins*, 1 Nob Hill, is another famous name for its architecture still includes some of the gables and turrets which were incorporated in the original mansion belonging to railroad magnate, Mark Hopkins. The *Fairmont*, on Nob Hill at California and Mason Sts was also originally the residence of another wealthy man – James Fair. Although the 1906 fire destroyed the majority of that mansion, it was rebuilt in good spirit.

Among the most elite hotels in Los Angeles are: the *Beverly Hills*, 9641 Sunset Blvd, a celebrated stop-over for stars and star gazers. Anyone who is anyone has to have a drink in the Polo Lounge here. The *Beverly Wilshire*, 9500 Wilshire Blvd, is less flashy but gathers a clientele familiar on the silver screen (if only to eat in its award-winning restaurant). *Bel-Air*, 701 Stone Canyon Rd, is a small, exclusive hotel in a lovely setting. Stars who prefer to keep themselves to themselves, stay here. In San Diego, the *Hotel del Coronado*, 1500 Orange Ave, on the Coronado Peninsula, is one of

America's grand old hotels. It was the country's largest wooden building when it opened in 1888 and other claims to fame include the fact it was one of the first ever hotels to instal electric lighting and lifts.

The 'resort hotel' is undoubtedly an American institution and one which works well. These are not city hotels although they may be near a city and the heavy emphasis is on sport and recreational facilities. The Golden West has plenty of these type of accommodations, but two worth mentioning are: *The Lodge at Pebble Beach* on the 17 Mile Drive, Pebble Beach. The setting is tremendous – the lodge is surrounded by Del Monte Forest, a private estate, where lodge guests can go horseback riding. There's swimming and tennis at the nearby beach club. The most popular sport at Pebble Beach, however, is golf – on the Pebble Beach Golf Links and the Robert Trent Jones-designed Spyglass Hill course. The *Santa Barbara Biltmore*, 1260 Channel Dr, Santa Barbara takes up 21 Montecito acres if you include the beautiful gardens. Luxurious guest rooms are housed in mission-style buildings and the property boasts an Olympic-sized pool and a quarter-mile beach.

Most of the ranch accommodations in the West are located in neighboring Arizona like *Tanque Verde Ranch*, 12 miles (19km) out of Tucson. Part of it used to be a stage coach stop and it is the last word in dude ranch luxury. In addition to the tennis, swimming, and health club facilities, supervised trail rides take place several times a day with a choice of 80 horses.

Lodges are a big part of the Californian accommodation scene for the state lays claim to 18 national forests, 17 wilderness areas and five national parks. Among them is the *Mineral Lodge* in Lassen Volcanic National Park; the *Giant Forest Lodge* in Sequoia; the *Grant Grove Lodge* in Kings Canyon; and the *Yosemite Lodge* in Yosemite Park.

Due to the vastness of the West's natural areas, camping is a much-loved pastime by Americans themselves. American campgrounds are some of the finest in the world, both for scenery and for facilities in case you don't like 'roughing it'. The parks all have campsites and anyone seeking solitude should explore the national park system. Organized camp trips with a guide and other campers, are also available. Useful addresses for these, in California are: *Yosemite Institute*, P.O.B. 487, CA 95389. (209 372 4441) Sierra Club, 530 Bush St, San Francisco, CA 94108, Tel (415 981 8634). Nature Expeditions International, 599 College Ave, Palo Alto, CA 94306. (415 328 6572). All the parks have an information center for visitors enquiring about available accommodations.

Other types of self-catering are possible in cottages or cabins in various parts of California. Many roadside motels' rooms have kitchenettes which are equipped with all the essentials. There are youth hostels throughout the States (with no age restrictions) but if you plan to use them, join in the UK first. Holiday apartments are generally not available on short let terms as they are in Europe, but a home exchange is possible with an American family.

Specialist resorts are scattered around California. One of the newest to gain popularity is the tennis ranch. The first *John Gardiner Tennis Ranch* is to be found in Carmel. It is small and luxurious and features a week-long clinic program between April and November, utilizing 14 plexiglass-surfaced courts. *La Costa Resort Hotel and Spa* in Carlsbad is one of those top notch spas with well developed tennis facilities – 25 hard-surface courts and a pro staff who give private lessons.

FOOD AND DRINK

Fresh fruit is very Californian – after all, it grows so well in the state's splendid climate. Oranges, strawberries, pomegranates, peaches – turned into juices, added to salads, flambeed with liqueur or served plain. Look out for dates, walnuts and avaocadoes as well. California is crammed with fruit groves, farms, and orchards and markets where they're all sold.

Owing to the availability of fresh vegetables, and the weather, salads are a favorite – as an appetizer, main course, or 'on the side'. A caesar or waldorf salad, for example, is often served as a starter. Spinach with bacon salad is a more than adequate lunch. In true American fashion, a full range of dressings is always available, but one of the most popular – green goddess – was invented in San Francisco.

Seafood is a Californian strength and it's all excellent. San Francisco, particularly, is renowned for its variety of seafood restaurants. Local shrimp are plump and meaty and may be bought by the carton from kiosks at Fisherman's Wharf, along with Dungeness crabs and clams. Several kinds of seafood go into *cioppino*, a sort of soup cum stew. When sole is on the menu, it's likely to be 'California rex' and if you've never tried abalone, this is the place. Red snapper appears on many a menu, cooked in a variety of ways and tuna may often be fresh. Monterey and San Diego are two other destinations noted for seafood.

Mexican cuisine is tops in California, especially in Los Angeles and San Diego where the *guacamole, tacos, tortillas,* and *frijoles* are just as authentic as they are south of the border. And naturally, there's always tequila to go with it.

With its history, it's not surprising that ethnic groups form large chunks of the state. Italians, Greeks, and Irish have all brought their culinary talents across the water with them so finding good European food in California is no problem at all. One of the largest ethnic groups is the Chinese. Both Los Angeles and San Francisco have a 'Chinatown', but Chinese food at its best is notable in San Francisco.

Nor can one visit the West without coming across masses of steak houses. Beef in all its varying cuts, but especially prime rib, is a ceaseless favourite throughout the state and portions are traditionally hefty. In fact decor termed as 'old San Francisco steak house' has been adopted all over the world.

When it comes to pies and pastries, you'll find Americans in general have a sweet tooth. Californians are no exception and a dessert list can be expected to feature such creamy concoctions as coconut cream pie, chocolate cream pie, lemon chiffon pie, and brownies (rich chocolate cake with nuts). Datenut bread and all kinds of muffins will be in the bread basket and don't miss sampling San Francisco's local sourdough bread.

The real Trader Vic's home is also San Franciso. Victor Bergeron may have travelled the globe leaving lovely Polynesian style restaurants behind him, but the original is on the Coast. For those unfamiliar with the Trader style, the decoration is all South Seas; the drinks are rum creations; and the food, an interesting mix of Malay, Indonesian, Chinese, etc.

Naturally, California boasts as many fast food outlets as the East, from fish and chips to over 50 kinds of hamburgers. Coffee shops, diners, kiosks, and takeaway food shops are all ideal for an inexpensive snack.

The drink in California (despite the fact it is claimed the martini was invented in San Francisco) is wine. It started at the missions with grape cuttings brought over by the Spanish padres. The cuttings planted at San Gabriel indeed became the basis of many Californian vineyards. Hungarian-born wine maker, Agnoston Haraszthy introduced Zinfandel grapes in 1851 at his Buena Vista vineyard, while French-born Etienne Thée and Charles Lefranc founded the Almaden vineyards

at Los Gatos, and Charles Krug started planting grapes in the Sonoma Valley in 1858.

Sonoma County is one of the state's big wine growing areas with over 12 wineries which welcome visitors. Highway 101 takes you right into Sonoma, home of those historic Buena Vista vineyards which were pioneered by Haraszthy. Although the original cellars were destroyed in the 1906 earthquake, they have since been restored. The winery is still operative (open 1000 – 1700) and a sampling may be made.

Further north, off Highway 101, are wineries in the Alexander Valley and the Russian River area. Perhaps the best known district, though, lies across the Mayacamas range – the Napa Valley, – where more than 20 wineries produce a delicious refreshment. The great wine road into the valley is State Highway 29. Along this highway between the city of Napa itself, and Calistoga, there's a string of wineries to be visited, like Inglenook (in Rutherford) Sterling (in Calistoga), Beringer (St Helena), The Christian Brothers (St Helena), Charles Krug, (St Helena), Robert Mondavi (Oakville) . . . which are among the best. The area itself is for sightseers, with its acres of vines, pine trees, and smattering of Victorian homes.

Another important wine centre is at Lodi, Sacramento. There are six wineries in and around Sacramento itself and only a short drive on State Highway 99 brings you to Lodi whose producers are famous for their wines and brandies. They have been particularly successful here in developing new grape varieties. Among the six offering tours and tastings are Coloma Cellars, East-Side Winery and the Winemasters Guild.

A further accessible wine area to be reached in a day from San Francisco is the Livermore Valley (over the San Francisco-Oakland Bridge and across the East Bay Hills on Interstate 580). The four wineries here include Concannon Vineyard and Wente Bros. Head south from Livermore and you come to Mission San Jose (Interstate 680), where a winery was founded by famous railroad builder, Leland Stanford.

Then there is the Santa Clara Valley where 20 wineries and tasting rooms are located. Take Highway 101 out of San Francisco going south – it should take about an hour. Paul Masson can be found at Saratoga, for example. In 2½ hours from San Francisco, you'll be in the community of San Juan Bautista (just east of 101), gateway to the vineyards of San Benito County. Almaden has a winery in San

Juan Bautista while in neighboring Monterey County there are new grape-growing areas to be admired and two tasting rooms in the city itself.

A helpful address when locating wineries in the Bay area is the Wine Institute, 165 Post Street in San Francisco – ask them for their booklet with directions.

Because of California's range of soils and climate, a surprising variety of wines are produced within the state. In many cases, they are similar to those of France, Germany, Spain, Italy, and Portugal, but equally they have a taste uniquely their own. In the range of whites, look for; Chardonnays, Chablis, Chenin Blanc, Sauterne, and Riesling. In the range of reds, look for; Burgundies, Zinfandel, Cabernet Sauvignon, Pinot Noir, and Gamay.

Really, the time of year to take a wine tour doesn't matter, as each season, California's wine country has its own special beauty. During the winter, the newly pruned vines appear stark, inside the wineries, the liquid is aging, occasionally being 'topped up' to replace evaporated wine and make sure the cooperage is completely full up. As aging progresses, the wine is 'racked' – transferred from one container to another. In the summer you can see minuscule grapes in the vineyards, gradually growing and ripening during the summer months.

Autumn is vintage time when clusters of grapes are picked and sent to be crushed. The juice is fermented with yeast and pumped into containers to start the aging process. White and rosé wine are left between six months and a year while the reds are often aged for four or five years before being bottled. A tour at this time of year will demonstrate unloading, crushing, and fermenting. And at all times of year, the visitor will see the casks, barrels, and tanks holding the aging wine.

ENJOY YOURSELF

Baseball The San Francisco Giants play pro-ball at Candlestick Park and Oakland Athletics at the Coliseum. (Professional football and basketball are also played in season at both these centers.) The Los Angeles Dodgers can be watched during the April–September season at 1000 Elysian Park Ave, a unique stadium that can accommodate up to 56,000 fans.

Boating There are splendid opportunities for all types of boating activity along the Californian coast from cruising to kayaks. In the San Francisco vicinity, Lake Merced and Lake Merritt along with the Bay itself are all good for boating.

Sightseeing cruises of the Bay leave from Pier $43\frac{1}{2}$, and from the adjacent docks for Alcatraz and Angel Island. Canoes, rowing and motorboats may be rented in Golden Gate Park for use on Stowe Lake.

Marina del Rey is a boating center for Los Angeles with thousands of yachts in the harbor and the Marina Belle which tours the marina daily. At any of the beaches on the city's doorstep, a variety of boats may be rented.

San Diego is idyllic for boat hire. Almost any kind of craft may be rented from San Diego and Mission Bay marinas. Lake Tahoe is another area favored by watersport enthusiasts.

Cycling California's national parks are some of the country's finest and a pleasure to cycle through along designated paths. Bikes can be rented at the lodges in the parks and at many of the resort hotels throughout the Golden West. Palm Springs, among other places, has routes specially marked for cyclists, covering 14 miles ($22\frac{1}{2}$km).

Canoeing One of the favorite spots for canoeists because it is safe all year round but fast enough to be interesting, is Russian River stretching for some 60 miles from Lake Mendocino Dam to the Pacific. Canoe rental is available from Burke's Russian River Canoe Rentals in Forestville.

Diving There's plenty of clear water out West for easy snorkelling and enough resort hotels and dive shops to rent out holiday equipment. Scuba diving takes experience and know-how, but for those who have it, La Jolla Cove in La Jolla is a recommended diving spot. It is part of the San Diego-La Jolla Underwater Park encompassing four miles of underwater scenery up the coastline to Torrey Pines. In addition to marine life, a huge submarine canyon is one of the best sights.

For information on sponsored diving expeditions, write: the National Assn of Underwater Instructors, POB 630, Colton, CA 92324, (714 824 5440). Or the Professional Assn of Diving Instructors, 2064 N. Bush St, Santa Ana, CA 92706, (714 547 6996).

Fishing An abundance of lakes, streams and rivers – as well as the ocean itself – provides a variety of fishing opportunities. Equipment and/or boats may be rented and chartered at any of the beach, resort and park communities. Salmon fishing at Monterey starts around mid February and lasts until September. San Diego's offshore waters are famed for ocean angling and party boats as well as special chartered boats operate on a regular basis from San Diego Bay, Mission Bay, and Imperial Beach. Expect to catch marlin and tuna in summer; rock cod and dogfish in winter. Albacore usually run July–October at La Jolla. Surf fishing is good between Imperial Beach and San Clemente. In the adjacent state of Nevada, you can find good fishing at Lake Mead and Lake Mohave.

Golf The Golden West is green with golf courses – it's one of America's favorite sports, and some of the courses are brilliant. Among the famous are the golf course at La Costa Hotel in Carlsbad; Pebble Beach Golf Links on the Monterey Peninsula plus nearby Spyglass Hill; Torrey Pines in La Jolla (where the Andy Williams tournament is held annually).

San Diego considers itself the golfing capital of southern California and, with 66 courses within the county, that's not so surprising. Most of them are open on a daily fee basis. One of the toughest is said to be Rancho Santa Fe (originally Bing Crosby's course). Palm Springs is another good golfing area with more than 35 courses to its credit.

Hiking Innumerable hiking trails, suitable to the novice and more experienced backpacker abound in the parks and forests. In Yosemite alone there are 700 miles (1126km) worth of trails, from short easy ones to overnight or longer tracks. For backcountry exploration, wilderness permits are needed, available on a first-come, first-serve basis, from ranger stations in the park.

Sequoia and Kings Canyon National Parks offer 500 miles (800km) of hiking trails and really the best way to enjoy the parks is on foot. Ranger-guided trips into the mountains and through the sequoia forests may be arranged at the Visitors' Center. One highlight trip is an 11-mile (17km) walk on the High Sierra Trail to Bearpaw Meadow. Other good hiking areas include Death Valley, Lake Tahoe, Redwood National Park, Lassen Volcanic National Park.

Hunting There is some hunting for duck, doves, quail, and deer in the Palm Springs region, and lots of hunting opportunities around San Diego. Provision is made for limited hunting in some of the national forest areas.

Horse Riding Stables where horses may be rented by the hour are found in all the resort locations, many times at large resort properties. In San Francisco, horse riding is available from Golden Gate Equestrian Center, Kennedy Drive at 36th Ave. Horse and mule packing are a High Sierra experience – offered in Kings Canyon and Sequoia National Parks. Such four-legged transport may be rented at Giant Forest, Grant Grove, Cedar Grove, Mineral King, and Owens Valley for pack trips. In Yosemite, there are stables at Curry Village and from Wawona campgrounds horses and mules may also be rented for guided one-day trips or anything up to six or seven-day trips.

Horse racing In Los Angeles, one can visit Santa Anita Park in Arcadia where the winter season lasts from late December to early April and in Autumn, the Oak Tree Racing sponsors racing. Another place is Hollywood Park at Inglewood where the thoroughbred season is April to July. Harness racing is held here from mid September until December. The season at Los Alamitos runs mid May to late August for watching night racing.

Bay Meadows is best in San Francisco for the horse racing set. Located in San Mateo, harness racing takes place here from the end of December to mid February; quarterhorse racing from late February to late May; and thoroughbred racing from early September to late December.

In San Diego, thoroughbreds race at Del Mar Race Track from July to September and also at Caliente Race Track, just over the border in Tijuana.

Mountaineering Climbing out West is good. In Lassen Volcanic National Park, the Lassen Peak Trail takes you on a 2½-mile (4km) climb to the top of Lassen Peak, and a popular climb in Sequoia and Kings Canyon parks will take you to the summit of Beetle Rock. Yosemite offers some exceptionally fine climbing and to make matters easier without being less challenging, contact the Yosemite Mountaineering School, which gives lessons on scaling the sheer valley cliff in the best way.

Sunday in the bay

Sailing Marina del Rey is supposedly the largest man-made small boat harbor to be found anywhere. Along with the choice of boat rentals, it features a sailing school – Rent-a-Sail, 13560 Mindanao Way, CA 90291. (213 822 1868). At Newport Beach, loads of sailboats are for hire while Sausalito is San Francisco's yachting center. Its marinas can hold a couple of thousand boats and lessons and or cruises are available from here.

Tennis California's 'in' sport. There are public courts, private tennis clubs and all the best hotels have their own. The newest thing is 'the tennis resort'. Many former pros have opened a string of their own like John Gardiner who has one in Carmel where you are determinedly instructed in hitting balls. It is called a Tennis Ranch, is luxurious, can take a minimal number of guests between April and November. La Costa resort is another in Carlsbad and so is the Vic Braden Tennis College in Trabuco Canyon if you're serious about the game. (The latter is not a place to stay but its facilities for improving the game are impressive.)

Many of the courts are night lit; of San Diego's 98 public ones, 70 are, and of Palm Springs' public courts (27), nine are. Tennis centres often feature automatic ball return practise lanes and video tape analysis, too.

Wintersports Closest wintersport region to Los Angeles is Big Bear and Lake Arrowhead. Yosemite is as good for pleasure seekers in winter as in summer. Badger Pass is used for downhill skiing while there are 90 miles for cross country ski use. Curry Village has its own outdoor skating rink. The area around Lake Tahoe offers excellent skiing; Heavenly Valley, Alpine Meadows, Northstar, Squaw Valley, and Kirkwood are first class resorts. An interchangeable lift ticket can be used for all of them. Heavenly Valley is a top resort in the area and very large. It is also the closest to the nightlife and quality hotels of South Lake Tahoe. Squaw Valley was a 1960 Olympic site so also offers something for everyone. Lassen Volcanic Park is first class for cross country skiing since almost all of the hiking trails can be used for this purpose in winter.

1984 Olympics
Tickets available in 1983 from the Los Angeles Organizing Committee, Los Angeles California 90084. (213 209 1984), Internat telex: 4720482.
Sites chosen at time of writing:
Archery at El Dorado Park in Long Beach where 2000 temporary seats will be provided and some 150 athletes are expected over the four days of competition.
Athletics nine days of field and track competition held at the Los Angeles

Memorial Coliseum (along with opening and closing ceremonies), whose capacity is 92,604. Some 1200 athletes are expected.
Basketball at The Forum in Inglewood, capacity 17,505. 216 competitors are anticipated over 12 days of competition.
Boxing at the Sports Arena next to the Coliseum, seating 16,353. Competition will last 13 days and should attract 400 boxers.
Canoeing and Rowing will take place on Lake Casitas near Ojai in Ventura County 750 rowers are expected and 350 canoeists – all of whom will be based at Santa Barbara. 10,000 temporary bleacher seats will be provided and spectators will be brought in from Los Angeles by private bus service.
Cycling at Cal State Dominguez Hills in Carson where a 333.3m velodrome is currently being built. Scheduled for five days of competition, it will have 2000 permanent seats and room for 6000 more temporary ones.
Equestrian at the Santa Anita race track in Arcadia. 100 riders are expected for nine days of events. The track has room for 25,000 spectators.
Fencing at the Long Beach Convention Center where there will be 6000 temporary seats. 400 athletes are expected for nine days of competition.
Football at The Rose Bowl with 104,000 seats. 272 players are expected for 10 days of competition.
Gymnastics at UCLA's Pauley Pavilion seating 12,500. 292 gymnasts should take part in 10 days of events.
Handball at Cal State Fullerton and Cal Poly Pomona. Fullerton's gym seats 4000; Pomona's, 4200. There will be 11 days of competition for an expected 270.
Field Hockey (not decided).
Judo at the Cal State Los Angeles gymnasium seating 4200. Some 270 competitors are expected for the seven days' competition.
Shooting (not decided).
Swimming the swimming and diving stadium at USC is currently being constructed with seating for 11,000. 600 competitors are expected for the 10-day event.
Volleyball at the Long Beach Arena, capacity 11,000. 13 days play and 216 athletes expected.
Water Polo (not decided).
Weight Lifting at Loyola Marymount University's Albert Gersten Pavilion presently being built. 300 athletes expected for the 10-day competition. Spectator capacity about 500.
Wrestling at the Anaheim Convention Center seating 7350. 600 participants for 10 days of events.
Yachting in the waters off Long Beach.

ENTERTAINMENT

Whatever you wish to find in the way of entertainment, you can find it in the Golden West. The range runs the gamut from Irish coffee parlours to strip and gay bars, from gambling to opera.

It is Las Vegas which calls itself 'Entertainment Capital of the World' and in many ways it is. It is certainly one of the few towns to be able still to afford top name performers and extravagant show-girl costumes. Caesar's Palace, the Sahara, and the Sands have obtained a reputation for presenting superstars. In the old days, the gambling paid for the entertainment to come free. Some of it still does in the cocktail lounges where lesser named artistes perform. But those big names do cost and do need reservations.

Most of the best nightlife revolves around hotels on The Strip where productions and sets are all lavish. The MGM, the Dunes, the Hacienda, and Tropicana are all nightlife leaders. A main hotel show room probably has an audience of between 800 and 1000 and usually features two shows: an early dinner show and a late drinks-only show. There is no cover charge *per se* but there will be a hefty minimum, generally covering a couple of drinks.

The best shows sell out quickly and a hotel's own guests get reservations priority so it's worth considering where to stay in advance. Reservations cannot generally be made until a day in advance. In addition to the floor shows, there are plenty of burlesque and topless lounges, discotheques, and piano bars.

It is the gambling, though, which entertains the majority. All the top hotels have their own casinos where almost every game of chance may be tried and those slot machines are located just about everywhere – including the airport! One of the most unusual casinos is at the Circus-Circus Hotel where a full scale circus takes place above the gaming tables, complete with sideshows. And the gambling, like the cabaret – keeps going until the very wee hours.

The after-dark scene in Los Angeles is a constantly changing one, just as it is in New York. New places come and go offering all kinds of entertainment to suit all kinds of people. Sunset Strip is not quite the way it used to be when stars in its clubs made the front page, but there's still enough going on with discos and folk music clubs, female impersonators and other clubs to choose from. Sunset Strip, with its topless nightclubs, its hawkers and mere passersby, is still fun.

One of the establishments which seem to have lasted is Doug Weston's Troubadour on Santa Monica Boulevard, which pioneered a number of rock music acts. (Blood, Sweat and Tears, for example were discovered here and the Smothers Brothers, among others, also used to appear. Santa Monica and Laguna Beach tend to be the trendier areas and for the Mexican fiesta spirit, it's Olvera Street downtown.

San Francisco's nightlife is just as promising whether one is looking for jazz or high camp, opera or strip. The main late-late area is around North Beach where the neon continually flashes, but all the hotels have at least one room featuring live entertainment and often a piano bar or singer in the lounge besides.

The city has acquired (unenviably or not depending upon one's view) a tag for being very 'gay'. There are indeed a fair number of places catering to that market, but a traditionally good establishment for female impersonations is Finocchio's on Broadway. It's been going a long time and has some of the best. If you're not into nude women wrestlers or love dancers, stay clear of Broadway and stick to downtown. Across the bay there are several good discotheques and jazz clubs.

San Diego's sleaze row is Lower Broadway – topless, go-gos, and all the etceteras. Nightlife in the large hotels and cosier bars of nearby La Jolla, is far classier. Or there's always the mariachi music of Mexico; Tijuana is just across the border, only 18 miles (28km) down the road from the center of San Diego.

Palm Springs is so resort minded that entertainment there is very good. Live music of some kind and/or disco can be found in all the top hotels, plus cabaret which in winter particularly may mean notable names. Piano bars are also very popular in this part of California.

On the cultural side, California has its strengths too. San Francisco is especially proud of its opera company which performs at the War Memorial Opera House and often features celebrated guest artists from mid September through November. Tickets are difficult to obtain so ensure advance reservations are made. The city's symphony orchestra also performs at the Opera House, with famous guest artists appearing from December through May. During the summer, there are sometimes free open-air concerts on Sunday afternoons. The San Francisco Ballet Troupe (America's oldest) can be seen at the Opera House December through May and in June during a summer festival.

Broadway style theater is staged at the Curran Theater along with musicals, and

Broadway shows are also put on at the Golden Gate Theater. Musical revues are presented at the On-Broadway Theater. Both classics and modern productions performed by the local rep company can be seen at the Geary Theater.

There is no shortage of theaters or music halls in Los Angeles, in all quarters of this spread-out metropolis. The Philharmonic plays at the Dorothy Chandler Pavilion, Music Center. Rock concerts take place at the Universal Amphitheater in Universal City; the New Greek Theater or the Roxy Theater. Los Angeles pro-rep company is based at the Mark Taper Forum's theater-in-the-round while tour-ing groups perform at the Ahmanson Theater at the Music Center.

San Diego's symphony and opera company are both based at the Civic Theater which is part of the Convention and Performing Arts Center. Rock stars are likely to play the Golden Hall (also part of the Center). The organ concerts on Sunday afternoons are free at the Organ Pavilion in Balboa Park. The city's answer to Stratford-upon-Avon, is its own Old Globe Theater where Shakespeare festivals take place in summer. Musical events can be seen at the Manderville Center and experimental plays, among others, are put on at Mission Playhouse.

YOUNG WEST COAST

One thing you can be sure of about the Golden West: there's plenty to keep the children amused, quite apart from the sand and sea. There are seaquariums and waxworks; ghost towns and restored old boats; film studios and zoos. If the kids are too young to appreciate culture and history and too small for the stamina needed to make the most of the scenic outdoors, take them to a theme park. Theme parks; or amusement parks, are an American speciality and there are plenty of good ones in California. Among the best are: **Disneyland** is the highlight for children of all ages, even those who look like adults! Many years ago, this Anaheim area was all orange groves. Now it is a continually expanding theme park where audio-animatronics (an invention of the late Walt Disney) bring storybook characters to life and thrill rides add to the pleasure.

There are currently seven themed 'lands': Adventureland, Bear Country, Fantasyland, Frontierland, Main Street, New Orleans Square, and Tomorrow-land. Each 'land' has its own attractions, priced differently and only sometimes free. There are five price categories, from A to E, an E attraction costing the most. Although you can pay as you go along, it's advisable to buy one of the ticket books at the entrance which contain varying numbers of coupons for all the categories. Ticket books also come in different sizes.

As soon as you make your way through the turnstile, you'll find yourself on Main Street bordered by shops – a street which could be, and was meant to simulate, any small town America main street. In old-fashioned Market House, 'penny candy' of the old-fashioned kind can be bought, and there are all kinds of gift shops including one which specializes in Disney character soft toys.

Main Street is the place you can take the Disneyland Railroad (D coupon), or one of the other yesteryear vehicles for a circuit of the main square (A coupon). Stop in to watch a silent film (B coupon). On the way down Main Street, you could well bump into Mickey Mouse (live) and certainly you'll pass an audio-animatronic figure of President Lincoln. During certain times of the day and year, parades and fireworks take place in this part of the park.

In Adventureland, 'Jungle Cruise' is a firm favourite with everyone (E coupon). The tour boat escort almost convinces the juniors that those hippos will overturn the boat – but, of course, like the bathing elephant and other animals seen along the way they are all audio-animatronically operated. Similarly, the birds and tiki gods are very lively in the 'Enchanted Tiki Room', a vine-covered South Seas Island hut (E coupon).

Leaving Adventureland, you'll arrive in New Orleans Square, a Disney-style French Quarter resembling the real one in New Orleans. Lacy grillwork balconies, courtyards, plants, and strolling jazz musicians add to the atmosphere. 'Pirates of the Caribbean' is located in this section – a ride which floats you in the dark into the land of pirates (E coupon). 'Haunted House' (E coupon) is equally popular, taking visitors on a spirit-world ride to meet the family as they pass from room to room.

In Bear Country, 'Country Bear Jamboree' (E coupon) is great fun or take the explorer experience in 'Davy Crockett's Explorer Canoes' (D coupon).

'Frontierland', as its name implies, shows the West as it used to be Disney-fashion, with mock gun fights and saloon revues. One of the freebies here is the

Disneyland's sailing ship

Sleeping Beauty's castle

stage show at the Golden Horseshoe. 'Mark Twain Steamboat' (D coupon) is very much in keeping with the frontier theme, plying its way along rivers and into Indian country. 'Tom Sawyer's Island' (D coupon) is reached by raft to explore its caves and tree house. The 'Columbia Sailing Ship' looks like an 18th-Century merchant ship and does its own cruise (D coupon), while the 'Mine Train' (D coupon) rolls past a lot of scenery in a short trip from mountains to a painted desert.

As you come to 'Sleeping Beauty's Castle', you're about to enter Fantasyland. 'Alice in Wonderland' features lots of familiar characters (B coupon) and 'It's a Small World' (E coupon) takes you on a slow-moving boat past masses of singing and dancing dolls all representing different countries of the world. Take a gentle spin on 'King Arthur's Carousel' (A coupon); a more rapid whirl on 'Mad Tea Party' (C coupon) or fly – in a 'Flying Elephant' (C coupon) or in a 'Peter Pan Flight' (C coupon). The section's most thrilling ride is 'Matterhorn Bobsled' (E coupon) which whips down mock ice slopes.

Tomorrowland is for the adventurous. 'Space Mountain' is probably the best attraction with its 'Mission to Mars' space trip (D coupon) and its 'Rocket Jet' (D coupon). Other features of this section are 'Submarine Voyage' (E coupon) and 'Adventure Thru' Inner Space' (C coupon).

Two final mentions are 'America Sings' (E coupon) in which more than 100 'animals' take part in four eras of music, and 'America the Beautiful', a free 360° screen film presentation. The park boasts all types of restaurant facilities but don't expect a scotch and soda – it's not Disney policy. Open daily in summer from 0900 – 2400 1313 Harbor Blvd, Anaheim. (714 999 4000).

Knott's Berry Farm is second only to Disneyland in the Anaheim area, and quite a Californian success story. It began in 1920 when Walter Knott, a farmer, opened a berry stand along Highway 39. Over a decade later, Mrs Knott started selling chicken dinners. Since then, the family affair has developed into a full-scale amusement park of 150 acres.

The major theme is the Old West. Ghost Town is the established favorite: take the stagecoach; be 'held up' on the train; pan for gold; or whip down a mountain in a hollowed-out log. Fiesta Village has a distinctive Mexican flavor and models of all the California missions. There's a Roaring Twenties section and the main feature of the Airfield is a 20-storey 'parachute jump'.

Throughout Knott's Berry Farm there are different eating places from food stalls to sit-down restaurants. Entertainment runs the gamut from fireworks and street acts to rock bands and top names in the park's theater. Country 'n' western artists frequently perform here and there's even an ice show on occasions. In summer, opening hours are 0900 – 2400 and sometimes later but it does close part of the week in winter. 8309 Beach Blvd, Buena Park. (714 827 1776).

Magic Mountain run by the Six Flags organization, experts on amusing diversions. The park is about 35 minutes by car from Hollywood (35mi/52km) via the Golden State Freeway. Nicely laid out with a special crafts area – Spillikin Corners – where glass blowers, wood carvers, and leather workers demonstrate their skills. The emphasis, however, is on the rides available. You can be whipped through the air, whirled, and twirled in a variety of ways.

Try the Log Jammer (hollowed out fiberglass logs) for a watery spill-thrill ride. It speeds through a mountain on a log flume course before plunging 47 feet (14m) into a lake. Rollercoasters come in all sizes: the Great American Revolution turns through a complete loop and The Colossus, a giant wooden roller-coaster, travels along two miles of tracks and drops 100 feet (30m) more than once.

Slightly less stomach-churning is the Metro Monorail; the Galaxy ferris wheel; air-jet-propelled skimmer boats; the Grand Carousel and the Sand Blasters (dune buggies). A sports car track and a gold mine train have their own circuits. In Children's World there are other rides suited to smaller youngsters plus a mini zoo and Wizard's Village. Magic Mountain has its own restaurant facilities that include the Four Winds on top of the mountain and a large theater that often features live entertainment. One admission price pays for all rides and amuse-

Knott's Berry Farm

ments. Summer hours are 1000 – 2400 daily, but in winter times do vary. Since Six Flags took over, a number of new puppet shows, dance revues. Full details from Magic Mountain, Valencia, CA 91355. (805 255 4100 or 213 367 2203).

No visit to The Golden West could be complete without calling on the movie industry. The younger film fans in the family will appreciate any one of the following places:

Movieland of the Air Museum will appeal to the boys in the family. It traces aviation history from its pioneer stage to modern space travel and also displays some of the planes from famous films. Visitors also have the opportunity to try a 'ride' in an open cockpit. Open daily in summer from 1000 – 1700. Closed Mondays in winter. Orange County Airport, Santa Ana. (545 5021).

Movieland Wax Museum is one of many attractions close to Disneyland, which is only a ten-minute drive away. A large number of film stars are represented here in some of their most famous poses, along with original props and 'sets'. Open Monday – Saturday 7711 Beach Blvd, Buena Park, (714 522 1154).

Movie World will please filmgoers with a penchant for cars. Most people call this Buena Park attraction 'The Home of the Cars of the Stars' because it has one of the largest collections of celebrity vehicles, displayed in their 'sets', to be seen anywhere. Open daily at 6290 Orangethorpe Ave (523 1520).

NBC Studios offers behind-the-scenes tours where you can watch 'sets' under construction, visit the wardrobe department, and see makeup artists at work. Sometimes, TV stars themselves can be seen as many top personalities tape their shows here. A limited supply of free tickets to NBC shows is available in the tour lobby. Tours run daily except Sunday, from 0900 – 1700. 3000 West Alameda, Burbank (213 840 3572).

Universal Studios is the world's largest studio site; 420 acres worth of mountain and valley and a tour of it should be top priority in the Los Angeles area. Take the guided tour of the 'sets' on a striped and canopied Glamortram and be prepared for some thrills along the way like a flash flood or shark attack. Who knows – something new is being dreamed up all the time?

During the tour, there's an opportunity to look in at some of the stars' dressing rooms and see some of the behind-the-scenes techniques for creating blood or rain, etc. At the end of the tour, visitors are shown round the Entertainment Center where there is a variety of film orientated amusements. In the Cinema Pavilion see the motion picture museum. In the Screen Test Theater, members of the audience can temporarily become 'stars'. Makeup artists and stunt men demonstrate their individual skills. Tours are continuous every day from 0800 – 1700 in summer and for the rest of the year, from 0800 – 1530. 100 Universal City Plaza, the entrance is at the junction of the Hollywood Freeway and Lankershim Blvd (213 877 1311).

Will Rogers State Historic Park depending on your age you may or may not remember the 1930s cowboy star, Will Rogers, with his homespun philosophy, trick riding ability, and rope tricks. This ranch, which was his home, is now supervised as a historic site and was once used as a hidaway by the Lindberghs after the murder of their first son. The house opens at 1000 but in summer the grounds stay open from 0700 – 1900. The admission fee includes an audio tour of the Rogers home. 14253 Sunset Blvd.

If you and your family enjoy the sea and its creatures you'll not be disappointed in The West Coast. There is a splendid aquatic park in Los Angeles and another in San Diego.

Marineland

Marineland is an excellent aquatic park where dolphins, whales, and sea lions are natural performers. Join a trained diver and snorkel in Marineland's special tank – and be watched via closed circuit TV by the non-diving members of your family. In the aquarium is a vast assortment of fish and other sea creatures. Open daily in summer but closed part of the week during winter months. Take the San Diego Freeway south to Hawthorne Blvd to get here or the Harbor Freeway south to its end. Palos Verdes Dr S., Rancho Palos Verdes (213 541 5663).

Sea World is an oceanarium in Mission Bay Park, San Diego, covering 80 acres. Several shows take place daily with dolphins, seals, and otters as stars along with

Shamu, a three-ton killer whale. Backstage, you can feed the dophins and learn how they're trained. There are sea life exhibits and rides here too. Open 0900 till dusk (714 222 6363).

One of the best zoos in the world is in San Diego but there are several other animal parks in Los Angeles featuring large animals and small docile pets as well. **California Alligator Farm** houses hundreds of reptiles, some of which are borrowed for TV and film performances. One of the largest crocodiles to be seen here weighs more than 1400lb (635kg) and is 15 feet (4.5m) long. Open year round from 1030 – 2100 during July and August; closing earlier for the rest of the year. 7671 La Palma Ave (714 522 2615).

Enchanted Village does enchant the kiddies. The Touching Place allows them to pet the animals or they can watch how they're trained and see them perform, even ride some. Open in summer daily from 0900 – 2100. Closed part of the week in winter. 6122 Knott Ave.

Lion Country Safari lets the wild animals (over 50 different species) roam freely, but you stay in your car. No convertibles are allowed in the preserve as a precaution against wandering rhino and cheetahs! Drive through the park at your own pace and rent a taped cassette if you wish. To reach Safari Country, take either the San Diego Freeway south, exiting at Moulton Parkway, or the Santa Ana Freeway to Sand Canyon exit. 8880 Moulton Pkwy, Laguna Hills. (916 837 1200).

San Diego Zoo is considered by many to be one of the world's finest because of the way it is designed. Very few of the 4000 animals housed here are actually caged. Tours of the 125-acre grounds can be made by guided tour bus or by the Skyfari Aerial Tramway which gives a bird's eye view of the lot. Among the most rare of the residents are New Zealand kiwis (believed to be the only ones kept in captivity) and the Indonesian Komodo dragon. The zoo has its own special children's section plus a theater where animal stars perform for

free. Open daily at Balboa Park (714 234 3153 or 714 231 1515). The Wild Animal Park, by the way, is a zoo development – an 1800–acre wildlife preserve where mini safaris among the 250 species are one of the features. Open evenings in summer, it is 30 miles (48km) north east on state route 78, off Interstate 15 at Escondido (234 6541 or 747 8702).

Among the other places of interest for the younger members of your family you will find a ghost town, a magnificent cruise liner, and a celebration of the conquest of space.

Calico Ghost Town is one of the most famous of the Golden West's ghost towns, half way between Los Angeles and Las Vegas (just outside Barstow on Interstate 15). In the 1880s, Calico was a boom town because of its silver mines. In 1881, three prospectors discovered a silver lode which produced $86 million in that metal over a 15-year period. Wyatt Earp often visited Calico in its best years. The Old West has been revived and you can still walk past the general store, the old schoolhouse, and saloon (714 254 2122).

Queen Mary is not just a great cruise liner but also a fascinating museum as well. The City of Long Beach purchased the vessel for $3 million and part of it is now being operated as a hotel. There are several restaurants and shops on board and Jacques Cousteau's Living Sea exhibit is one of the best of its kind. Permanently moored at Pier J, the *Queen Mary* is now classed as 'a building'. Open daily and reached via the Long Beach Freeway (213 435 4747 or 4733).

Rueben H. Fleet Space Theater simulates space travel. Far more sophisticated than the usual planetarium, this one uses images projected on a 360° screen – thousands of stars on the theatre dome perhaps or a duplicated trip to the moon. Science-minded youngsters will also enjoy the exhibits on astronomy in the Science Center here, where there are laser demonstrations on weekends. Open daily. Reached off Park Blvd, in San Diego's Balboa Park. (714 238 1168).

Queen Mary, *Long Island*

SHOPPING

Ghirardelli Square, San Francisco

American shops are so tempting as to be almost irresistible. Large department stores like May Company, Bullock's, Robinson's in Los Angeles are crammed with goodies. Boutiques are liberally sprinkled all over the state, often trendy and often pricey (as in Beverly Hills). Cleverly designed shopping complexes, often converted from factories or warehouses, such as San Francisco's Ghirardelli Square or The Cannery, are a pleasure just to browse round. Ethnic shopping can be fun, too, for example in San Francisco's Chinatown where a host of Oriental merchandise may be purchased.

Clothing is always a good buy in the US. California manufactures and sells excellent resort and leisure wear and the range of sizing and colours is far better than in British shops. Linens are also a worthwhile purchase for the choice of patterns and colours, at prices well below English ones for the equivalent. Look at towels for the same reason.

Tapes and records are generally cheaper while gimmicky items and computerized games, etc. are frequently available in US stores long before they reach the UK. Fad conscious California is overall good for buying 'amusing'

souvenirs. Soft toys are a bargain – look for the name 'Dakin' (a Californian company which makes delightful cuddly animals). Disneyland shops have lots of 'character' soft toys. Baby clothes are another consideration – lots of choice at low prices for tiny babies.

Since supermarkets are the first choice for food shopping, the markets (like Farmer's Markets in Los Angeles) have become attractions. Unusual jellies, jams, and chutneys can often be found at the market stalls for a present that's different, while dates and nuts are almost invariably cheaper than at home.

Gift shops are literally everywhere, carrying a wide range of merchandise that starts off with toothpaste and ends up with cut crystal. (Drug stores – chemists – often have a gift section.) Wherever there's a tourist attraction, you can be sure of one or more places to make purchases.

The main downtown shopping area of San Francisco is in and around Union Square (where there's a branch of New York's famous Macy's). Shopping malls are housed in the Embarcadero Center which covers 8½ acres between the financial district and waterfront. Around midday, street vendors set up stalls of handcrafted goods that include leather

Fisherman's Wharf, San Francisco

items, jewellery, and macramé. Main thoroughfare of Chinatown is Grant Avenue if you're opting for things Oriental.

Down at Fisherman's Wharf is the fun place to shop. Ghirardelli Square used to be a chocolate factory once upon a time. Imaginative conversion has turned it into a shop and restaurant complex that everyone wants to see. The goods for sale come from all over the world and it's open daily. The Cannery originally was where tinned fruit and vegetables were manu-

factured – definitely not as chic as it is today with its three levels of boutiques and eating places, surrounding a pleasant central courtyard, where street musicians entertain shoppers. It, too, is open daily.

Just east of Fisherman's Wharf but still on the waterfront is San Francisco's newest (well, at the time of writing) shoppers' mecca – Pier 39. The complex was rebuilt with the wood from other demolished piers in the vicinity and houses a variety of stores and restaurants plus a children's playground.

In Los Angeles, it will be hard to know where to start first, but it could be at Olvera Street where the city first began. In this pedestrian zone are Mexican shops, restaurants and food stalls in keeping with Los Angeles history.

Shopping malls are to be found in every quarter of Los Angeles (as indeed they are throughout California). They are undoubtedly an American institution and are designed in 'open' and 'closed' varieties. Open malls are of obvious benefit, since regardless of the weather (too hot, too cold, too wet), they are pleasant to browse through. Most of them house branches of major department stores along with boutiques and eating areas. One well-landscaped mall in Los Angeles is Los Angeles Mall – the first mall to be built on City Hall property. The Arco Plaza on South Flower St boasts seven below-ground acres of shops and the Broadway Plaza is a two-level underground mall below the Flower St Office Building and the Hyatt hotel.

Things to buy and things to eat go together. Farmer's Market at Fairfax and Third St concentrates on foodstuffs, both fresh and cooked, at its fruit and veg. stalls, takeaway stands and in its patio restaurants. But you'll also find such nonperishable goods here as straw goods, jewellery, and wooden carvings. In New Chinatown, between North Broadway and North Hill St, happi-coats, ivories, fans, and pottery are as plentiful as the *dim sum* (Chinese savoury snacks).

Some of the complexes are more chic than others. For example, Fishermen's Village at Marina del Rey recreates a New England fishing village, a good place for small gift items, while Port of Craft at the Venice edge of Marina del Rey comprises a cluster of boutiques on the brink of a canal, specializing in arts and craft items. The smart and well-established Lido Village in Newport Beach features rows of shops which open onto bricked walkways or front the boating wharf. Another Newport Beach rendezvous is Cannery Village which stretches for five blocks along the wharf, where old houses and stores have been revitalized and artists' stalls have been added. And more artisans (of all kinds) can be found in the Whole Earth Market Place on Ventura Blvd in Encino where an old supermarket has been converted into a fun gathering place.

Olvera Street, Los Angeles

Ports o' Call Village, San Pedro

One of the best-known complexes for gift selections is Ports O'Call and Whaler's Wharf in San Pedro. The former achieves a Mediterranean seaport effect with the aid of brightly hued plants and flowers and in the latter, all the stores and taverns are fashioned in colonial style.

The Los Angeles answer to Portobello Rd (for antiques, at least) is Melrose Ave, between Fairfax and La Cienega Blvds. Actually, it's a lot more tasteful for this once purely residential street utilizes patios and gardens as well as the properties themselves.

The most famous shopping mecca is Beverly Hills – to be precise, Rodeo Drive. But be warned – the goods have the best labels, the prices are astronomical.

THE LANGUAGE

There is a language difference, although with a little practice it is easily overcome. It still can cause amusement and even raised brows in some quarters. For instance, if you go about knocking someone up, you're in dire trouble – that's Americanese for *making pregnant*. And if you're looking for a rubber, do please try to remember it's an *eraser*, and cotton is *thread* and cotton wool is *cotton*.

It shouldn't take long to acquire a basic understanding for simple situations. When the telephone line is engaged, for example, it's *busy* and if you wish to make a reverse charge call, ask to make it *collect*. When the barman asks if you'd like your drink *on the rocks* or *straight up*, what he's trying to enquire is would you prefer it with ice, or neat!

Similarly, a pavement becomes a *sidewalk*; a lift, an *elevator*; and a flat, an *apartment*. (Their *studio* apartments are like our bedsits only much much better.)

A *purse* could be a purse – on the other hand, it could be a handbag, which is really a *pocketbook*. If you're wearing a *vest*, it's not what you think it is, but a waistcoat. And if you really want to foil an American, tell them you brought your anorak (*ski jacket*) with you. Wear a *pin* and it's not to hold up a droopy hemline – it's a brooch.

If you're taken short on the highway, you'll find clean *restrooms* (toilets) at the *gas station* (garage), but don't call them loos – they're *johns*. While you're there, you may as well fill up with *gas* (petrol). Should the attendant ask you to raise the *hood*, he does mean bonnet and, of course, windscreen wipers are the same as *windshield wipers*. Both buses and coaches, by the way, are referred to as *buses*, unless the old-fashioned 'stage' variety of coach is meant, but if you're told to watch out for the *truck*, do – it's a lorry. Sometimes even simple words get changed around. For rubbish, say *garbage* and for luggage, *baggage*.

Accept a *canapé* and it's still an hors d'oeuvre although on some menus, an *entrée* refers to a starter, not a main course. A sweet may be a dessert but if you were hankering after the chololate bar/toffee variety, request some *candy*. *Biscuits* are sort of scone cum muffin but certainly not McVities which take the name of *cookies*.

Occasionally, food will have to be judged by its looks. Who, after all, would guess that *zucchini* are really courgettes? Or indeed that aubergine is revealed to be *eggplant*. Fruit and veg. come in *cans* not tins, and *jelly* is jam. (Jelly for dessert is *jello*.) Coffee with *cream* probably only means milk (a *regular coffee*).

A chemist is a *drug store*. Post becomes *mail*. Ask the *janitor* (caretaker) to fix the *faucet* (tap) but a *bellhop* (hotel porter) to carry packages. Take the *subway* (tube) for fast transport and watch *soccer* if you want to see football played with a round ball.

WHAT YOU NEED TO KNOW

Airports Los Angeles International Airport is about 18 miles (29km) from the central business district. Limousine, bus, and taxi services are available into town. San Francisco International Airport is located about 13 miles (21km) southeast of the city. Las Vegas' McCarran International Airport is only eight miles (13km) from downtown.

Banks Basically 0900 – 1500, although some banks in the major cities have later hours on certain days of the week.

Churches Churches of all denominations are found in the large cities. Local papers list services and hotels will direct guests to those closest.

Climate Regionally variable. San Francisco can be cool and misty even in summer – and it does rain. Los Angeles can be stiflingly hot in summer but San Diego has an idyllic climate year round. Palm Springs and Las Vegas are always hot, but the latter benefits from low humidity and a dry desert air.

Clothing For all destinations, informal casual clothing is the right day wear, except for San Francisco where people tend to be a little dressier. At night, especially in winter, Palm Springs dresses up and evening in top Las Vegas resorts can bring out the sequins.

Consulates For southern California, the British Consulate to contact is the one located at the Ahmanson Center East Building, 3701 Wilshire Blvd, Los Angeles CA 90010. (213 385 7381). For travellers to other parts of Nevada and northern California, the consulate is in the Equitable Building, 120 Montgomery St, San Francisco, CA 94104. (415 981 3030).

Credit All major credit cards, American Express, Diners, Visa and Mastercharge (Access), are accepted by a wide range of hotels, restaurants, and stores throughout the Golden West.

Drinking The legal drinking age is 21 although Nevada tends to have a rather freer policy. Bar opening and closing times vary not only with state but with municipality but you'll find a drink any hour of the day or night somewhere.

Electricity The standard supply is 100 volts, 60 cycles AC.

Emergencies Dial 911

Gasoline Cheaper than in the UK, but sold in US gallons. 1 US gallon is equivalent of about ⅘ of an Imperial gallon or 3¼ litres.

Handicapped America as a whole is well up on facilities for the handicapped, from special highway rest areas to lift buttons in braille. The Central Bureau for Educational Visits and Exchanges, 43 Dorset St, London, W1. (01-486 5101) should be able to help with specific information and The Royal Assn for Disability and Rehabilitation, 25 Mortimer St, London, W1 (01-637 5400) has its own holiday officer.

Health All doctors in the US are 'private' so health insurance for overseas visitors is essential as charges are very high. Anyone on prescription medicine should take what they consider to be a sufficient supply with them, plus the actual prescription.

Postage Some main post offices remain open 24 hours a day. Otherwise, usual hours are 0800 – 1800 Monday – Friday and 0800 – 1200 on Saturday. Closed Sunday. Stamps are available at the desk in better hotels, or from vending machines (but you pay over the odds for the stamp you require), in drug stores, train, and bus terminals etc. Don't confuse post boxes with litter bins – they are somewhat similar in shape, and nothing at all like British pillar boxes.

Public Holidays New Year's Day (1 Jan.); Washington's Birthday (third Mon. in May); Memorial Day (Last Mon. in May); Independence Day (4 July); Labor Day (first Mon. in Sept.); Columbus Day (second Mon. in Oct.); Veteran's Day (11 Nov.); Thanksgiving (4th Thurs. in Nov.); Christmas Day (25 Dec.).

Rabies, unfortunately, is widespread in the Golden West. Caution is essential when approaching any wild animals, or dogs roaming free from control. There is at present no effective preventive vaccine against rabies. A bite or scratch incurred through contact with a wild or stray animal should be washed immediately with soap and water, and medical advice should be sought. Any animal being imported into the US must have a valid certificate of vaccination against rabies.

The UK totally prohibits importation of animals (including domestic pets) except under license. One of the conditions of the license is that the animals are retained in approved quarantine premises for up to six months. No exemptions are made for animals that have been vaccinated against rabies. Penalties for smuggling involve imprisonment, unlimited fines and destruction of the animal.

For details apply to the Ministry of Agriculture (Animal Health Division), Hook Rise South, Tolworth, Surbiton, Surrey KT6 7NF.

Shopping Store hours vary but the regular times are 0930 or 1000 – 1730 or 1800 Monday – Saturday. Large stores will open at least one night a week, probably to 2100 and some may open on Sunday. Food stores usually open at 0900, drugstores earlier. Some delicatessens and groceries will open on a Sunday in the major cities.

Tax State and city taxes are added to the retail price of goods displayed in shops and to meals in restaurants.

Telephones Public telephones can be found on the street, in hotel lobbies and drug stores, restaurants, terminals and gas stations etc. Exact coinage is required on all direct-dial calls. A reverse charge call is known as a 'collect call' and costs nothing. (The initial local charge is immediately refunded.)

Time Both California and Nevada are on Pacific Standard and Daylight Savings Time (about eight hours earlier than London time).

Tipping In restaurants which don't add a service charge, 15 – 20 per cent of the bill is expected. Taxi drivers expect at least 15 per cent of the total fare as a tip and porters, from 50¢ to $1 per case. As with everywhere else, a tip for special service is customary.

Toilets The standard of cleanliness is very high in public toilets (rest rooms). There should be no worries using any at gas stations, diners or in designated rest areas along the highway.

FESTIVALS AND EVENTS

Greater Los Angeles

January; Pasadena Rose Bowl football game and Tournament of Roses Parade, Winston Western 500 Stock Car Race, (Riverside).

February; Glen Campbell Open Golf Tournament, Camellia Festival (Temple City), Black History Month, Carrot Festival (Holtville), Chinese New Year, Festival of Whales (Dana Point), National Date Festival (Indio), Whiskey Flat Days (Kernville).

March; Azalea Festival (South Gate), Clairol Crown Tennis Classic (Rancho La Costa), Dinah Shore Winners Circle Golf Tournament (Rancho Mirage), Return of the Swallows (San Juan Capistrano), Long Beach Grand Prix, World Championship Gold Panning (Buena Park).

April; Colorado River Country Fair (Blythe), Conejo Valley Days (Thousand Oaks), Heritage Days (Bakersfield), Lilac Festival (Palmdale), International Film Exposition, Tournament of Tennis Championship (Carlsbad), Multicultural Festival (Oxnard), National Mime Week, Pan American Festival (Lakewood), Spring Festival (Lone Pine), Western Days (Lakeside), Wildflower Festival (Wilmington).

May; Cinco de Mayo, Desert Tortoise Days (California City), Early California Days (Fillmore), Frontier Days (Lake Elsinore), Grubstake Days (Yucca Valley), Heritage Days (Lancaster), Long Beach International Festival, La Ballona Valley Days (Culver City), La Fiesta (San Luis Obispo), May Festival (Orange), Monrovia Days (Monrovia), Mule Days (Bishop), National Orange Show (San Bernardino), Old Fashioned Days (Altadena), Potato & Cotton Festival (Shafter), Roundup Days (Adelanto), San Fernando Fiesta, Strawberry Festival (Garden Grove), Western Days (Valley Center), World Trade Week, Sidewalk Arts Festival.

June; Cherry Festival (Beaumont), Festival of Friendship (Lincoln Heights), Hesperia Days (Hesperia), Off-Road Championship Grand Prix, Olive Festival (Sylmar), Semana Nautica Sports Festival (Santa Barbara), Winston Cup Stock Car Race (Riverside).

June/July; Southern California Exposition (Del Mar).

July; Asian Cultural Festival, Coca-Cola Superbowl of Motocross, Eastern Sierra Tri-County Fair (Bishop), Festival of Arts (Laguna), Old Miners Days (Big Bear Lake), Orange County Fair (Costa Mesa), Santa Barbara County Fair (Santa Maria).

August; Farmers Fair (Hemet), International Karate Championships (Long Beach), International Surf Festival, Long Beach Sea Festival, Nisei Week, Old Spanish Days Fiesta (Santa Barbara), San Bernardino County Fair (Victorville), San Fernando Valley Fair (Northridge), San Luis Obispo County Fair, Santa Monica Sports & Arts Festival, Off-Road World Championships (Riverside), Tehachapi Mountain Festival (Tehachapi), World Body Surfing Championships (Oceanside).

September; Antelope Valley Fair & Alfalfa Festival (Lancaster), Basque Festival (Chino), Danish Days (Solvang), Desert Empire Fair (Ridgecrest), Festival of Roses (Wasco), Fiesta de la Luna (Chula Vista), Harvest Festival (Littlerock), Hispanic Heritage Week, Kern County Fair (Bakersfield), Los Angeles City Birthday, Los Angeles County Fair (Pomona), Morongo Valley Fiesta Days (Morongo Valley), Oktoberfest (Big Bear Lake), Pow Wow Days (Apple Valley), Valyermo Fall Festival (Valyermo), World Championship Beach Volleyball (Redondo Beach).

October; Artesia Parade (Artesia), Borrego Daze (Borrego Springs), Budweiser Grand Prix (Riverside), Calico Days (Yermo), Early California Days (Wofford Heights), Fall Harvest Festival (Julian), Festival of Masks, Frontier Days (Canyon Country), Golden Days (Azusa), Goleta Valley Days (Goleta), Irvine Harvest Festival (Irvine), Stagecoach Days (Banning), Tiller Days (Tustin), Ventura County Fair, Wine & Harvest Festival (Delano).

November; Chrysanthemum Festival (Artesia), Hollywood Christmas Parade, Mother Goose Parade (El Cajon).

December; City of the Christmas Story (Santa Monica), Dickens Downton Christmas, Las Posadas.

Monterey

January; Bing Crosby pro-amateur Golf Tournament.

February; Winter dressage competition.

March Carmel Kite Festival.

May; Adobe House Tour.

July; Feast of Lanterns.

August; County Fair.

September; Festival of Santa Rosalia.

San Diego

January; Andy Williams Open Golf Tournament.

February; Jack-in-the-Box Invitational Indoor Track Meet.

March; Pacific Coast Men's Doubles Championships, Beach Kite Festival, Honda Civic Golf Classic. Torrey Pines Soaring Contest.

Easter; Mission Bay Easter Egg Hunt.

April; San Diego Crew Classic. Tournament of Champions, Lakeside Family Fair, Ramona Pageant, Jumping Frog Jamboree.

May; San Ysidro Cinco de Mayo Celebration, Maytime Band Review, Western States Music Tournament, Valley Center Western Days, Fiesta de la Primavera, Shakespeare National Festival.

June; Jazz Festival, Model Yacht Regatta, Camp Pendleton Rodeo, Corpus Christi Fiesta, Old Town Art Fiesta, La Jolla Tennis Championships.

July; Independence Day Celebrations, God Bless America Week, World Championship Over-the-Line Softball Tournament, Junior World Golf Championships, Sun 'n' Sea Festival, Festival of the Bells,

Mission San Luis Rey Fiesta, Trek to the Cross, Mission Bay Sand Castle Contest.
August; America's Finest City Celebration, Carnation Festival.
September; Thunderboats Race, Cabrillo Festival.
November; Annual Fiesta de la Cuadrilla, Harvest Festival.
December; Mission Bay Parade of Lights, Old Town Christmas Parade, Old Town Posada, Christmas Light Boat Parade.

San Francisco
January; National Sports and Boat show.
January/February; Chinese New Year Festival.
March; St. Patrick's Day Parade, Livestock Exposition & Horse Show.
Easter; Macy's Easter Flower Show, Easter Sunrise Services, Mt. Davidson.
April; Nihonmachi Cherry Blossom Festival, Yachting Parade.
May; Bay to Breakers Race, Master Mariners Regatta.
June; Union St Spring Festival, Upper Grant Ave Street Fair, San Francisco Birthday Celebration, Midsummer Music Festival.
July; 4th July Celebration.
August; San Francisco County Fair Flower Show.
September; San Francisco Municipal Outdoor Art Festival, Japanese Fall Festival, Transamerica Open Tennis Championships.
October; Blessing of the Fishing Fleet, Grand National Livestock Exposition, International Ski & Winter Sports Show.
November/December; Dickens Christmas Fair.

USEFUL ADDRESSES

Automobile Club of Southern California, 2601 S. Figueroa St, Los Angeles 90007. (213 741 4311).
Car rental Budget Rent a Car, 9775 Airport Blvd, Los Angeles 90045. (213 645 4500). California Parlor Car Tours, 350 S. Figueroa St, World Trade Center, Ste. 130, Los Angeles 90071 (213 625 2448). Gray Line Tours, 1207 W. Third St, Los Angeles 90017. (213 481 2121). Lounge Car Tours, 21133 Victory Blvd Ste. 205, Canoga Park 91393. (213 340 4803). Trailways, 1501 S. Central Ave, Los Angeles 90021. (602 742 1222). VIP Limousine Service, Los Angeles. (213 273 1505).
Cruises Catalina Cruises, Catalina Terminal Berth 96, San Pedro 90733. (213 775 6111). Channel Island Cruises, POB 3709. Beverly Hills 90212. (213 274 3025).

Long Beach Catalina Cruises, 330 Golden Shore Blvd, Long Beach 90802. (213 832 4521). Santa Catalina Island Sightseeing Tours, POB 737, Avalon 90704. (213 510 2500). Western Cruise Lines, 140 W. Sixth St, San Pedro 90371. (213 548 8411).
Information American Express (Destination Services), 723 W. Seventh St., Los Angeles 90017. (213 488 1331). Greater Los Angeles Visitors & Convention Bureau, 505 S. Flower, Los Angeles 90071. (213 488 9100). Anaheim Area Visitor & Convention Bureau, 800 W. Katella Ave, Anaheim 92803. (714 999 8999). Beverly Hills Visitors Bureau, 239 S. Beverly Dr, Beverly Hills 90212. (213 271 8174). Big Bear Lake Valley Chamber of Commerce, 520 Bartlett Road, POB 2860, Big Bear Lake 92315. (714 866 4601). Bishop Chamber of Commerce, 690 N. Main, Bishop 93514. (714 873 8405). Buena Park Visitor & Convention Bureau, 6696 Beach Blvd, POB 5308, Buena Park 90622. (714 994 1511). Escondido Visitors & Information Bureau, 720 N. Broadway, Escondido 92025. (714 745 4741). Goleta Valley Chamber of Commerce, 5902 Calle Real, Goleta 93017. (805 967 4618). Hollywood Chamber of Commerce, 6290 Sunset Blvd, Suite 525, Hollywood 90028. (213 469 8311). Las Vegas News Bureau, Convention Center, Las Vegas 89105, (702 735 3611. Long Beach News Bureau, 300 E. Ocean Blvd, Long Beach 90802. (213 436 3645). Oceanside Chamber of Commerce, 510 Fourth, Oceanside 92054. (714 722 1534). Oxnard Convention & Visitors Bureau, 325 Esplanade Dr, Oxnard 93030. (805 485 8833). Palm Springs Convention & Visitors Bureau, Municipal Airport Terminal, Palm Springs 92262. (714 327 8411). Ridgecrest Chamber of Commerce, 301-A S. China Lake Blvd, POB 771, Ridgecrest 93555. (714 375 8331). Riverside Visitors & Convention Bureau, 3443 Orange, Riverside 92501. (714 787 7950). San Bernardino Convention Center, 303 N. E, San Bernardino 92418. (714 383 5245). San Diego Convention & Visitors Bureau, 1200 Third Ave, Suite 824, San Diego 92101. (714 232 3101). Santa Barbara Chamber of Commerce, 1301 Santa Barbara, POB 299, Santa Barbara 93102. (805 965 3021). Santa Ynez Valley Advertising Council, POB 173, Solvang 93463. (805 688 6210). Ventura Visitors & Convention Bureau, 785 S. Seaward Ave, Ventura 93001. (805 648 2075). San Francisco Convention & Visitors Bureau, 1390 Market St., San Francisco 94102. (415 626 5500). Trans Catalina Airlines, 19300 Ike Jones Rd, Santa Ana 92707. (714 557 7276).

MUSEUMS AND GALLERIES

Los Angeles

George C. Page Museum not long completed to house the restored Rancho La Brea fossils (which were found on the adjacent site). Altogether there are 500,000 specimens in the collections which include a replica of the skeleton of the only human remains discovered at La Brea; skulls of the dire wolf; fossils of giant vultures, mastodons, even camels! The Rancho La Brea (tar pits) site in Hancock Park proved to be a rich source of Ice Age fossils when scientists began to study it at the beginning of the century, and even more so when the current excavation started in 1969. Tours of the tar pits are given Thurs. – Sun. from 1000 – 1700 when visitors can learn the ecological significance of the excavations besides seeing some of the techniques which were used to uncover the fossils. Visitors may also look in on the 'dig' from the Page Museum, where the Pleistocene (Ice Age) Mural shows the animals as they would have been when they lived in those times in the Los Angeles Basin. 5801 Wilshire Blvd, (213 936 2230). Open Tues. – Sun. from 1000 – 1700. Admission charge.

Grauman's Egyptian Theater lies just across the street from the more famous Chinese Theater and was another showy masterpiece. It was designed to resemble an ancient palace of Thebes and used to be the setting for jazzy film premieres in the great days of Hollywood. Unfortunately, the studio extras dressed as Arab sheiks don't walk the ramparts any more and the usherettes, looking like Cleopatra, aren't around. 6712 Hollywood Blvd.

Henry Huntington Library and Art Gallery was once the home of the railroad tycoon. Huntington was a devotee of fine artworks and great books as his collections here will testify. The art gallery's most famous painting is Gainsborough's *Blue Boy*, but also of note are Gilbert Stuart's portrait of George Washington, Sir Joshua Reynolds *Sarah Siddons as the Tragic Muse*, and Romney's picture of Lady Hamilton. The house has a number of decorative arts, handsome furniture, and Beauvais and Gobelin tapestries.

There are both permanent and changing exhibitions in the library. Of particular interest among the British and American first editions is a copy of the Gutenberg Bible printed in the 15th century; a 1410 copy of Chaucer's *Canterbury Tales* and a first folio of Shakespeare's plays. Benjamin Franklin's original hand-written autobiography and Edgar Allan Poe's handwritten copy of 'Annabel Lee' may also be seen among the several million manuscripts in the collection.

Within Huntington's 207-acre estate are some well-planned botanical gardens. Cacti in all shapes and sizes grow in the Desert Garden; over 1000 varieties of camellia grow in the Camellia Garden and dwarf maple trees, reflection pools, and a bonsai court give the Japanese Garden an authentic ambience. 1151 Oxford Rd, San Marino. (792 6141). Open Tues. – Sun. 1300 – 1630.

Hollywood Wax Museum anyone who *was* anyone, and indeed *is* anyone, on the silver screen is represented in life-like poses in this famous waxworks. The Beatles are there and so is Marilyn Monroe in her celebrated dress-blowing scene from *The Seven Year Itch*, not to mention Mae West, and Glen Campbell is among the contemporaries. The museum features its own Chamber of Horrors with scenes and items from famous horror films. In the Oscar Movie Theater you can view years of Academy Award winners. 6767 Hollywood Blvd, (213 462 8860). Open daily 1000 – 2400, (Fri. and Sat. until 0200). Admission charge.

J. Paul Getty Museum is sometimes referred to (sarcastically) as 'Pompeii by the Sea'. Located on a ten-acre Getty estate near Malibu, it is a reconstruction of a Roman villa and houses the Getty collection. His main interest was in Greek and Roman sculpture, but the museum's decorative arts section primarily features 18th-century French furniture and tapestries. The painting galleries contain Italian Renaissance and Netherland baroque works but also include Georges de la Tour's *The Beggar's Brawl* and Raphael's *The Holy Family*.

The museum is surrounded by a colonnaded garden with a reflecting pool and bronze statues. Open summer Mon. – Fri. 1000 – 1700 and winter Tues. – Sat. 1000 – 1700 (454 6541).

J. Paul Getty Museum, near Malibu

Los Angeles County Museum is the biggest and the best in the state. There are three pavilions. One features constantly changing exhibitions. The second, the Leo S. Bing Theater, gives weekly lectures and concerts and often, film presentations. The third, the Ahmanson Gallery, is a mix of ancient and modern exhibits. In the sculpture garden there are works by Moore and Calder among others. 5905 Wilshire Blvd, Los Angeles, CA 90036. (213 937 4250). Closed Mon. and some public holidays. Open Tues. – Fri. 1000 – 1700; Sat. & Sun. 1000 – 1800. Admission charge.

Mann's Chinese Theater is not a museum in real terms, but it's a Los Angeles freebie that simply can't be missed. For many years it was known as Grauman's Chinese Theater (after showman Sid Grauman). The latter imported Oriental temple pillars for it. Stars who really are stars have always been invited to make an imprint of their hand or foot in wet cement in the forecourt, or write their signature. Shirley Temple did; Elizabeth Taylor did; Paul Newman – and many, many more. Some even went further: Betty Grable left an imprint of her leg and Gene Autry, the hoofprints of his much-loved horse. 6925 Hollywood Blvd.

Chinese Theater, Los Angeles

Natural History Museum has over 35 halls and galleries with pre-history to present-day exhibits. The Mayan, Aztec, and Inca works are exceptional. Other exhibits vary from the arts and crafts of the South Pacific to fossils of extinct creatures, and the works of photographer Edward S. Curtis who spent his life ensuring the American Indian customs and traditions didn't become a lost heritage. 900 Exposition Blvd. Closed Mon. Open the rest of the week from 1000 – 1700, Admission free.

Norton Simon Museum of Art used to be the Pasadena Art Museum before it was taken over by the Norton Simon Foundation in 1974 and revitalized. The galleries feature 19th- and 20th-century art works plus stone and bronze sculptures from India and Southeast Asia. Possible the best of the Chola bronzes on view is the Sivapuram Nataraja from the 10th century, which shows the Hindu god Siva as Lord of Dance. Among the major paintings to be seen are works by Rubens, Rousseau, Matisse, Corot, Picasso, and Breughel. Colorado Blvd at Orange Grove. (449 3730). Open Thurs. – Sun. 1200 – 1300. Admission fee.

The Southwest Museum has a wealth of American Indian relics. The museum was founded by Charles Lummis, director of the Los Angeles Library, in 1907. He gave his own fine collection of rare books on the Southwest plus a large archaeological collection to the museum. On display are all types of Indian artifacts and paintings plus the story in pictures of Chief Sitting Bull along with a painting he did himself on a canvas liner of a US cavalry blanket shortly before he was assassinated. Open Tues. – Sun. from 1300 – 1645. 234 Museum Drive, Highland Park.

Forest Lawn is the cemetery satirized by Evelyn Waugh in *The Loved One*. Whatever one thinks, it has become a tourist mecca, particularly the Great Mausoleum where celebrities like W.C. Fields, Jean Harlow and Clark Gable are entombed. In the Mausoleum is a *Last Supper* window based on Leonardo da Vinci's painting. It is displayed in the Memorial Court of Honor at 1000 – 1100 and half hourly from 1200 – 1600, and is the work of Rosa Moretti, the last in line of an Italian family noted for its secret process of making stained glass.

Forest Lawn has its own museum which holds a reproduction of Ghiberti's Paradise Doors among other things. In the theater next door, two paintings are displayed every half hour from 1100 – 1700. One of these paintings, '*The Crucifixion*' is supposedly the largest permanently mounted painting in America. Most of the statuary in Forest Lawn are reproductions of world-famous pieces such as Michelangelo's *David* which stands in the Court of David.

The memorial churches in the grounds are worth inspecting, too. In the wing that adjoins the Church of the Recessional, Rudyard Kipling's family album and mementos are on view. The church itself simulates a 10th-century English church just as the Wee Kirk o' the Heather resembles a 14th-century Scottish church. The latter features a stained-glass window portraying the life of Annie Laurie. 1712 South Glendale Ave, Glendale. 0900 – 1700.

San Francisco

Cable Car Museum shows you all you need to know about this unique form of transportation. In the car barn at Washington and Mason Sts. Open Apr.–Oct. 1000–1800; Nov.–Mar. 1000–1700.

California Academy of Sciences is the West's oldest science institution. Until 1906 it was housed in several downtown buildings and after the city's big fire was moved to its present location. The Hall of Mammals is in the North American Hall (west wing) displaying American mammals in natural settings. The Hall of Birds also houses a huge collection and the Hall of Minerals exhibits a host of geological items.

More than 12,000 fresh and salt water fish can be seen in the Steinhart Aquarium. There are also tanks for dolphins, piranha and talking fish plus an alligator swamp in the entrance court.

The first star projector to be installed anywhere in America is a feature of the Alexander F. Morrison Planetarium (East Wing). Star shows are given afternoons and evenings. In this same wing of the Academy is The Science Museum and Simson African Hall. The evolution of the clock is presented in the Science Museum along with a lamp collection that ranges from primitive times to present day. The Alice Eastwood Botanical Collection is also to be found here. Simson African Hall houses animals hunted by Leslie Simson, a mining engineer and sportsman who presented his trophies to the museum. Golden Gate Park. Open 1000 – 1700. (415 752 8268)

Chinese Wax Museum portrays in gory detail the murder of Chinatown's notorious vice king – 'Little Pete' (who started the Tong war in his ten year reign of terror). At Grant and California Sts.

The M.H. De Young Memorial Museum is one of America's greats and certainly one of the largest in the Golden West. The original museum came into existence thanks to the successful exposition, but since then was replaced wing by wing. Among the wealth of art masterpieces to be seen here are Rubens' *Tribute Money* and El Greco's *St John the Baptist*.

There are changing exhibits in the East Wing whereas those in the Central Wing are a permanent collection of European and American arts. The West Wing is of particular note as it contains the history of San Francisco. All the wing is dedicated to California and includes a comprehensive costume collection from 1760 to present

times, 19th-century room settings, model ships, and items relating to shipping. The Armor Room in the same wing houses a world-wide weapon collection.

The Avery Brundage collection wing looks out over the Japanese Tea Garden and accommodates a fine Oriental display. Golden Gate Park. (415 752 5561). Open 1000 – 1700. Admission charge.

Palace of the Legion of Honor is dedicated to the dead of World War I and is modelled after the Palais de la Légion d'Honneur in Paris. It has both a scenic location and one of the finest art collections on the West Coast. The emphasis is on French paintings and sculpture in the permanent exhibitions and most of the changing displays are devoted to modern art. Rodin is especially well represented since he was a friend of the museum's donor. Among his works to be seen are the original bronze of *The Burghers of Calais*, *St John the Baptist* and one of the original five bronze casts of *The Thinker*. Lincoln Park. (415 752 5561). Open daily 1000 – 1700. Admission charge.

National Maritime Museum displays all things nautical for free. You'll find a host of fascinating ships' figureheads, anchors, and bells; a good model ship collection; plus the photographic history of San Francisco's waterfront. Beach St at the foot of Polk. Open daily 1000 – 1700. Just east of the museum, for a small fee, one can board several restored Californian vessels including a three-masted lumber schooner.

Museum of Modern Art is the city's third major art museum. It concentrates on showing contemporary artwork from around the globe. Among the famous names are Picasso, Klee, and Pollack, but a fair sampling of the work of local living artists is also housed here. McAllister St. Open Tues., Wed., Fri. 1000–1800, Thurs. 1000=2200, Sat., Sun. 1000–1700.

Palace of Fine Arts, San Francisco

THE MISSIONS

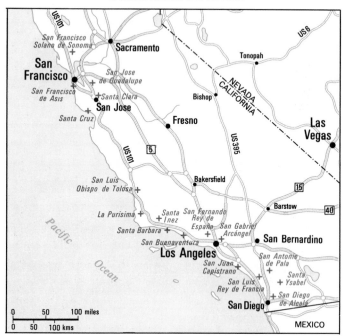

The mission system, set up by the Spanish, was an early form of colonization. Eventually, a chain of 21 missions was established between San Diego and Sonoma. the first nine were founded by Father Junipero Serra. Early missions were little more than mud huts and only later were they built of stone in the adobe style which we associate with 'mission architecture'. Not all of them remain in existence, and one, San Rafael, has disappeared without trace but those which can be visited are, from south to north:

San Diego de Alcalá was originally founded in 1769, the first of the mission chain, on Presidio Hill. It was moved to its present site in 1774 in order to use a good water supply. Restored in 1931, it is open to the public daily from 0900–1700 and services are held every Sunday in its chapel. Taped guided tours are available. At the Father Luis Jaime Museum, there are several relics of early mission days, including Father Serra's own handwritten mission records. 10818 San Diego Mission Rd, San Diego (714) 281 8449).

San Luis Rey de Francia was founded in 1798 by Fermin Francisco de Lasuén and is located four miles (6.5km) west of Oceanside in San Diego. Often referred to as the 'King of Missions', it was the largest and one of the loveliest. It once housed almost 3,000 Indians and some of their original paintings are still on view. Services continue to be held here and the mission puts its museum are open daily for self-guided tours from 0900–1600. 4050 Mission Ave, San Luis Rey (714 757 3651).

San Antonio de Pala was built in 1816 as a branch of Mission San Luis Rey. Its museum contains Indian artifacts and is open Tues.–Sun. from 0900–1500. Located on Highway 76, near Mt Palomar (714 742 3317).

Santa Ysabel was founded in 1818 to assist San Diego de Alcala and contains a museum, murals, and an Indian burial ground. Open daily from 0900 to dusk. Located on State 78, near Julian about 33 miles (40km) east of Escondido (714 765 0810).

San Juan Capistrano was a mission pueblo founded in 1776 by Fermin Francisco de Lasuén and known as the 'Jewel of the Missions'. It features unusual gardens and a gold altar, a diorama of early mission life and the original bells of Campanario. It is also the celebrated summer home of the swallows. Open daily from 0700–1700. Ortega Highway at Camino Capistrano (714 493 1111).

San Fernando Rey de España was founded in 1797 by Fermin Francisco de Lasuén. Completely restored, it boasts seven acres of grounds and shows many examples of Indian and Spanish architecture. Open daily from 0900–1600. 15151 San Fernando Mission Blvd., Mission Hills, Los Angeles (213 361 0186).

San Gabriel Arcángel was founded by Serra in 1771. Its church (built in 1805) is famed for its bells and its museum contains prime examples of early life in California. Open daily 0930–1600. 537 W. Mission Dr, San Gabriel, Los Angeles (213 282 5191).

San Buenaventura was the last mission to be established by Father Serra (in 1782) and is Ventura's pride and joy. Open Mon.–Sat. 1000–1700 and Sun., 1000–1700. 211 E. Main St, Ventura (805 648 4496).

Santa Barbara founded in 1786 by Fermin Francisco de Lasuén and known as 'Queen of the Missions'. It is one of the most beautiful missions, notable for its twin towers. Remains of an original aqueduct system have been located on the grounds. Open Mon.–Sat. 0900–1700, Sun, 1300–1700 at Laguna and Los Olivos Sts, Santa Barbara (805 682 4713).

Santa Ines founded in 1804 by Estevan Tapis and is often called 'Mission of the Passes' or 'Hidden Gem of the Missions'. A major restoration programme has made this one of the most impressive attractions in the Santa Ynez Valley – with a museum, interesting murals in its church, and a peaceful garden. Open daily 0900–1700 in summer and in winter 0930–1630. 1760 Missions Dr, Solvang (805 688 4815).

La Purisima founded in 1787 by Fermin Francisco de Lasuén and now in a state historical park. The restored grounds and buildings show all the aspects of mission life. Open daily 0800–1700. Purisima-Casmalia Rd, Lompoc (805 733 3713).

San Luis Obispo de Tolosa is a mission pueblo founded by Serra in 1772 and called the 'Princes of Missions', its name being taken from St Louis of Toulouse, a prince who became a bishop at 16 and died aged only 24. The three 1820 bells are still in use. Open daily 0900–1700 in summer and to 1600 in winter. 782 Monterey St, San Obispo (805 543 6850).

Santa Cruz was originally founded in 1791 by Fermin Francisco de Lasuén but was destroyed in an earthquake in 1857. All you can see today is a half-sized reproduction, but it does include original furnishings from the altar, the statues, and vestments. Mission Hill, Santa Cruz.

Santa Clara was originally founded in 1777 by Tomás de la Peña, but was destroyed three times. The present building is a fourth reproduction and is the chapel of the University of Santa Clara. Whatever items were saved from the earlier buildings are now here, like the redwood cross in front of the chapel which dates from 1777. Other items include fonts and wooden statuary.

San Jose de Guadalupe was founded in 1797 by Fermin Francisco de Lasuén and became one of the leading missions despite a number of troubles with Indians and the natural elements. The only portion of the original buildings remaining today is a large common adobe room housing items from the mission's past, including vestments worn by the founders and bells cast in 1815 and 1826. Open daily from 0900–1700. Located 15 miles northeast of San Jose on State 17 (415 656 9125)

San Francisco de Asis is better known as Mission Dolores. It was founded in 1776 by Father Serra but construction of the present building was started in 1782 in adobe style. It took on the name 'Dolores' because of the Spanish name given to a nearby lake – Laguna de Nuestra Senora de los Dolores. The mission's crypts and adjacent graveyard are full of early San Francisco history. Open daily from 1000–1600. Located at Sixteenth and Dolores Sts, San Francisco. (415 621 8203)

San Francisco Solano de Sonoma was the last mission to be established, in 1823. The present building is a restoration. Its museum contains part of the Bear Flag staff, hand wrought iron hinges from Fort Ross and a number of papers of historical importance to California. Open daily from 1000–1700.

San Luis Obispo

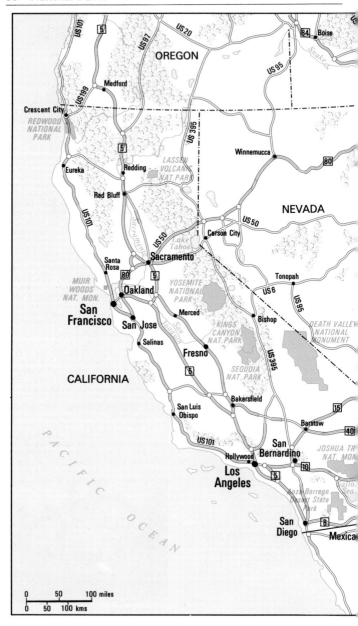

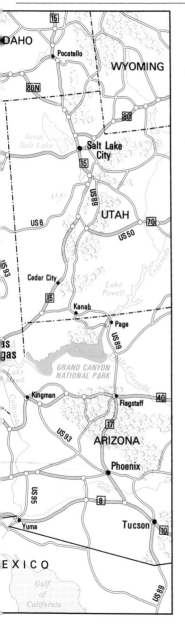

NATIONAL PARKS

The Golden West is especially rich in natural conservation areas, many designated as national parks. Almost all of them can offer camping and lodge accommodation, hiking trails, and ranger programs. The headquarters of the National Park Service will provide brochures on all the area parks if enquiries are addressed to their Information Services Dept., Interior Building, Washington D.C. 20240 (202 343 4747).

Grand Canyon National Park, Arizona, is one of the world's most awe inspiring natural wonders. Despite the fact that from the canyon's rim, the Colorado River flowing along the floor is not always visible and when it is, appears to be little more than a thin stream, from the canyon floor, a mile below the rim, the river looks what it is, mighty!

The river began eroding layers of sediment a million odd years ago. Once upon a time the whole area was flat but over the aeons, wind, heat, and pressure formed mountains. The latter were eroded with time, formed again, eroded into deserts, and covered by shallow sea. All this natural history is visible by studying the canyon itself since multiple layers of rock, of varying colours and texture, form 'steps' from top to bottom of the chasm. The first ledge at the bottom of the canyon is formed by Precambrian black shiny rocks which are among the oldest exposed on earth.

Each layer is of a different composition and hue with fossil remains between them. The sheer cliffs of Redwall limestone, a grey-blue limestone deposit, are 500ft (150m) thick and show examples of amphibian and fossil ferns. The Cocino sandstone above comprises the solidified remains of sand dunes in which there are fossilized lizard footprints. The best fossil evidence of the area's geological history can be seen in the top layer of Kaibab limestone – fossil sponges, shark's teeth, and corals are among the evidence that a shallow sea once covered the land.

Together, the layers have created 'a sculpture' of incomparable magnificence which stretches for 277mi (446km); at its narrowest point it is four miles (6.5km) across, and at its widest, 18mi (29km) wide, with a depth of one mile (1609.3m). As one might imagine, there are several vantage points and a host of trails for the adventurous hiker. The motorist will have to drive 200mi (322km) to cover the distance between the South and North rims whereas the hiker will only be travelling 21mi (34km). The Kaibab Hiking Trail, however, is a tough one and only recommended for the experienced.

To get oriented, go first to the South Rim Visitor's Center where the Yavapai Museum and Tusayan Ruin and Museum will give you an introduction to the canyon's history. The Center itself will provide information on daily and weekly activities which usually include ranger-guided nature walks along the rim plus more rugged excursions into the canyon.

South Rim drives extend for 35mi (56km), with several lookout points along the way. Cars aren't allowed along the eight mile (13km) West Rim drive during the summer, but a free shuttle bus services the key points en route, throughout the day from early morning. The best canyon view is from the West Rim. Ranger stations are located at Hopi Point, Mohave Point, and Pima Point, from all of which talks are given on geology, botany, animal life, and the peoples of the Grand Canyon.

Hiking trails into the canyon also start at the South Rim, like the Bright Angel Trail which has rest facilities at 1½ and 3mi (2.4–4.8km) and the steeper South Kaibab Trail. You can join an organized hike or, of course, you can go it alone, but remember the canyon's at its hottest in the middle of the day so bring along protective gear and leave plenty of time for your return journey. The South Rim is the more popular with tourists as it has the most facilities. In addition to the campgrounds are the Bright Angel Lodge and the Yavapai and Thunderbird Lodges.

There are two easier ways of exploring the canyon – by air on a scenic sightseeing flight, or by mule. If you take the latter mode of transport, there are one day or overnight rides. If you take to the air, you may need your travel sickness tablets – the planes are small and the warm air currents from both sides of the gorge can make the flight a little choppy.

Being less accessible, the North Rim is always less crowded, yet its setting and views are superb. For the best lookout point, take the 26mi (42km) Cape Royal Drive to Point Imperial, which at over 8,000ft (2438m) is the highest point on the canyon's rim. From here, you can look across the Painted Desert, Marble Canyon and obtain an impressive view of the Colorado River. Geology talks are given at Cape Royal and there are campfire programs at the campsite near Grand Canyon Lodge. Another tremendous panorama can be seen from Toroweap

Point, down 3000ft (900m) of sheer cliff. Don't try any of the North Rim ventures in winter – heavy snow closes the area. The accommodations in this part of the canyon are North Rim Inn and Grand Canyon Lodge plus the camp site. The most luxurious place to stay within the park is El Tovar at South Rim, a renovated old hotel with a good dining room and fantastic canyon views from some of the balconied suites. Because of the popularity of this natural wonder, any accommodation reservations should be made well in advance. Information from the park's superintendent at Grand Canyon, AZ 86023 (602 638 2411).

Lassen Volcanic National Park contains one of America's most recently erupted volcanoes, Lassen Peak. When, after centuries of peace, it spurted steam and lava in 1914, it continued to do so for seven years. The park itself is one of California's smallest in the national system, but exciting – like a miniature Yellowstone – with its bubbling mud pools, boiling springs, and steamy holes called fumaroles.

The park headquarters are in Mineral, on State 36 (turn off Interstate 5 at Red Bluff) a few miles from the entrance where a Visitor's Center provides information. A second Visitor's Center is located at Chaos Crags, some 35mi (56km) east of Enterprise which is on Interstate 5. Between the two centers runs the 30mi (48km) Lassen Park Road which meanders through the western portion, containing all major sights.

A host of hiking trails lead to the thermal areas. If you take the Lassen Peak Trail, it's a 2½mi (4km) climb to the top, but an easier hike will take you at Bumpass Hell, the largest hot spring area with nearby Little Hot Springs. Big Boiler, Steam Engine, and the Sulphur Works. Although in many ways the park is best visited in summer when all the roads are open, it is in this south western part that winter skiing takes place.

Most rugged section of the park is in the east. To reach it take pack trips or horseback rides starting from Summit Lake. Camp sites and lodges are located in the vicinity of Manzanita Lake, open only in summer. From this resort area, visitors can take the Lily Pond Trail to Reflection Lake. Among Lassen's attractions are Cinder Cone (in the northeast corner) which became a national monument before the land became a park. Stark as this black cylindrical cone is, the surrounding 'Painted Dunes' – colourful volcanic ash formations – make up for it. Every name in Lassen tells a story from 'Devastated Area' where the lava flows

Grand Canyon

stripped the life and a forestry program had to be introduced to revitalize it, to Dwarf Forest where small conifers struggle to get bigger. These days, at least for the moment, Lassen and Cinder Cone are dormant once again. Information from the park's superintendent at Mineral, CA 96063 (916 595 4444).

Mineral Lodge (open in winter) is *the* place to stay. Facilities include a pool and tennis and a mountain view.

Redwood National Park is as its name suggests, a park full of giant redwood trees. Within it are three state parks: Jedediah Smith State Park close to Crescent City, the location of the park's Visitor's Center; Del Norte Coast Redwoods State Park, also near to the Center; and Prairie Creek Redwoods State Park, not far from the southern boundary and Orick – entry point for anyone travelling from San Francisco.

The world's tallest trees, up to 300ft (90m), can be found along Redwood Creek. Although similar to (and indeed related to) the Sequoias, redwood trees are a darker red and have thinner trunks. So many redwoods have been cut down over the decades for furniture, that those in this park are some of the remaining few. They have suffered from their advantages: durability and fire-resistance.

Prairie Creek State Park is full of giant redwoods and due to a heavy rainfall, is green with other foliage besides. Moss and lichen have turned the 50ft (15m) high Fern Canyon walls emerald while herds of elk indulge themselves in the meadows of the Madison Grant section of the park. Campsites can be found at Gold Bluffs where jagged promontories jut out into the sea, and at Prairie Creek, but anyone looking for a comfortable motel should head for US 119 or 101.

In spring, the Dalmatian Trail which winds down the coast of Del Norte Coast Redwoods State Park, is aflame with azaleas. In this section, virgin redwood forest extends to the rocky shore and camping sites are located at Mill Creek. The largest trees in Jedediah Smith State Park grow in the Frank Stout Memorial Grove whose 340ft (103m) Stout Tree is a big attraction. Camping facilities plus swimming and a beach are situated along Smith River.

The redwood groves are peaceful and darkened (their topmost interlacing branches practically form a 'roof', blocking out much of the light). A number of hiking trails inside the park lead to the bluffs overlooking the Pacific and May–Oct. is the most worthwhile season for a visit. Park information from Crescent City, CA 95531 (707 464 6101).

Sequoia and Kings Canyon National Parks are administered as one park, a gateway to Southern California's Sierras. Together they offer a 65mi (104km) stretch of natural scenery, dominated by the USA's highest peak, Mt Whitney, 14,495ft (4418m). Travel by car and you do see the giant sequoias, for which the park was named. But the proper way to see the parks is on foot or by mule. Indeed, there are only two major roads – the one open year round only traverses the south western corner.

Should you drive, use the beautiful Generals Highway, a 50mi (80km) section of State 198, beginning southwest of Sequoia not far from the town of Three Rivers. This route will take you through all the most majestic sequoia stands before joining State 180 to enter Kings Canyon. The world's greatest examples of sequoia will be passed along the way, all named for American generals. The tallest is General Sherman Tree which is 272ft (83m) high and over 106ft (32m) thick and estimated to be some three and a half thousand years old. Giant Forest not far away contains sequoias in all stages of development, from tiny saplings to huge ancients.

Another notable tall tree is General Grant Tree (267ft/81m) in Grant Grove just inside Kings Canyon, which is six feet (2m) thicker than Sherman. Robert E. Lee Tree is nearby and the area's fourth largest sequoia is Hart Tree in Redwood Mountain Grove, west of Generals Highway in Sequoia National Forest.

Stop at Lodgepole Visitor's Center on Generals Highway to view exhibits on the trees and the rest of the park's aspects. This ranger station will give you all the information on available park activities. There are information centers in Grant Grove and Cedar Grove, but Lodgepole is the starting place for guided hiking and backpacking excursions. Such trips can be organized at the center as can bookings for campsites and cabins.

One of the park's most imposing sights is Moro Rock (in the vicinity of Lodgepole). From here (it rises 6,725ft/2050m) there is a magnificent view of the Great Western Divide. Crescent Meadow and Tharp's Log which was the 19th-century log cabin headquarters of explorer Hale Tharp, are both a short walk away. See also Beetle Rock (best climbed late in the day) and Crystal Cave whose unusual limestone formations are explained by park rangers.

To reach Bearpaw Meadow will require an overnight trek but the scenery along the 11mi (17km) of High Sierra Trail is well worth it. This trail continues past Bearpaw east to meet Muir Trail at

Wallace Creek. Side trips from here will take you to Mt Whitney, Big Arroyo and Kern Canyon.

In Kings Canyon Park, start hiking from Cedar Grove (which boasts a campsite). The least explored areas are in the heart of the park where there are mountains and lakes galore. Discover the region on foot or by mule.

In addition to the number of campsites in both parks, there are stores and supply centers with provisions for hikers. They also sell the necessary fishing licenses. For pack trips, mules and horses may be rented at Giant Forest, Grant Grove, Cedar Grove, Mineral King, and Owens Valley. Information from the superintendent of both parks at Three Rivers, CA 93271 (209 565 3341).

Yosemite National Park is probably California's grandest and most exciting national park, encompassed as it is by the majestic Sierra Nevada mountains – 250mi (402km) of them along the Nevada border. It became California's first state park mainly due to campaigning by early conservationist, John Muir, who discovered that glaciers had cut the valley from the rocky Sierras. Thanks to him its unparalleled natural beauty has been preserved. It is, as Muir described it, 'the finest piece of divine architecture'.

Yosemite Valley is the big attraction, a piece of meadow and forest land seven miles (11km) long by one mile (1.6km) wide fed by the Merced River. From the valley floor, granite walls rise as high as 4,000ft (1200m). The world's largest known single block of granite is right here – El Capitan – a sheer unfractured 3,500ft (1066m) wall that can only be climbed by experts. It is not the only Valley landmark. Across from it rise the 2,700ft (323m) Cathedral Spires and on the northern side are the Three Brothers, three peaks that lean against each other to a full height of 4,000ft (1200m). The upper valley widens into a semi circle of granite domes known as Sentinel Basket, North Dome, and half Dome.

Cascading waterfalls are another outstanding Yosemite feature, the highest of

Yosemite

Sequoias in Yosemite

Death Valley

which is Yosemite Falls, plunging a total of 2,425 spectacular feet (739m). But also see Ribbon, Bridalveil, Nevada, Vernal, and Illilouette Falls. Glacier Point, reached by a winding road through pine forest and meadow and only open in summer, offers a panoramic vista and is also a park highlight. Hikers may take the Four Mile Trail, a steep zigzag path to the valley floor or the Pohono Trail which is longer but easier as it encircles the rim.

The Valley's activity center is Yosemite Village where camping and other lodging, shops, and restaurants are available. The Visitor's Center here provides information on ranger-guided walks and lectures and a free shuttle bus tour of the valley can also be taken.

Highest alpine meadow in the High Sierra is Tuolumne, an 8,600ft (2621m) gateway to the high country. During the summer months the campground here is open and a naturalist programme is in operation. Of Yosemite's three giant sequoia groves, the Mariposa is the largest. A couple of hundred of those beautiful redwoods grow in the grove, each ten foot or more in circumference.

Lovers of the outdoors couldn't do better than Yosemite. The choice of trails for hiking is such that it doesn't matter whether you're a novice or veteran, but to travel in the back country, one does need a special permit issued by any of the ranger stations. Saddle trips or short-duration mule trips can be organized through the stables at Curry Village and Wawona Campgrounds. Curry Village and Yosemite Lodge also rent out bikes – another good way to enjoy the park. Would-be climbers are advised to contact the Yosemite Mountaineering School. In winter,

while many roads are closed, Curry Village remains a holiday centre. It has its own outdoor skating rink and there are 90mi (145km) of trails for cross-country ski use and the Badger Pass for downhill skiing. The season runs from mid December to early April with equipment available on its slopes. The runs are mostly suited to beginner and intermediates.

The best and most famous of Yosemite's lodging is the Ahwahnee Hotel which was built in 1927. Though rustic, it is de luxe enough to require dressing for dinner – a meal which could very well comprise salmon or prime rib. This hotel will arrange hiking or rock climbing for its guests in summer and skiing or snowshoeing in winter. Open year round, it indulges in a special amount of pageantry at Christmas. More park information from the superintendent, P.O.B. 577, Yosemite National Park, CA 95389 (209 372 7726).

In addition to the national parks, the Golden West has many other natural splendors. Among those are:

Anza-Borrego Desert State Park was named for de Anza who crossed this burning stretch of land on his way from Mexico to Monterey. Legend has it that he and compatriots were directed by an angel to find water. Legend? Mirage? Or the rock which can be seen today shaped like an angel with outstretched arms towards Coyote Canyon and the waters of Coyote Creek?

Situated 90mi (145km) northeast of San Diego, much of this half million acre park remains as wild as it was in Spanish settler days. The main center is Borrego Springs from which visitors can take an easy circular 40mi (64km) trip. On the way, stop at Font's Point for the view of the Borrego Badlands where chasms are gashed from towering granite walls. And at Palm Canyon where hundreds of desert palms grow.

Ranger-guided tours are available and there are several campsites within the park, best of which are at Agua Caliente Springs and Vallecito State Station. Blair Valley, on the southern route, is open all year round.

Death Valley National Monument is the third largest of America's national monuments, covering a 3,000sq mi (7770 sq km) area, some of which is well below sea level. It is in fact one of the world's hottest, lowest, and driest places. Death Valley lies 140mi (225km) west of Las Vegas off US 95 and 300mi (483km) northeast of Los Angeles on State Routes 14 and 190, and owes its name to the gold prospecting party who got lost and died in the valley during the Gold Rush era.

What today is a dramatic sightseeing excursion was in the past a terrible obstacle to overcome before reaching California. Those 'forty-niners' thought they had discovered a quicker route when they hit upon Death Valley – they were wrong! Even today, summer temperatures have been as high as 135°F. For something unusual, stand at Dante's Viewpoint from where you can see the lowest point in the western hemisphere at the same time as the highest point in the continental US (Mt Whitney).

One of the odd phenomena found here is the pupfish or 'desert sardine' which has adapted to the high temperatures and thrives. It is one of several species not found elsewhere but which flourish in the Death Valley streams. And springs and streams there are despite the heat and the annual rainfall of less than two inches. There's even a lake and small swamp. Of course, in ages past, Death Valley was the floor of an inland sea and sections of sand dunes are today's evidence of a former inland seashore. You can see a bed of salt crystals, another remnant, and what is known as the 'Gnome's Workshop' is an area of odd salt formations which remained after the sea evaporated.

At one time Death Valley's mines were sources of wealth. Boom towns were built with names like Skidoo. The mines and towns are no more, though visitors will see mining center remains on their way to the Visitor's Center at Furnace Creek which offers slide shows and lectures. Horses may be rented from here or you can take a self-guided tour by car.

Among the highlights are Zabriskie Point, Titus Canyon, and Telescope Peak, over 11,000ft (3350m) high, plus the valley's lowest section, Badwater. You will find campsites at Bennett's Well, Furnace Creek, Mahogany Flat, Mesquite Spring, Midway Well, Sunset Campground, and Texas Spring, but you can't reserve in advance. The main tourist season lasts from mid autumn to mid spring, when temperatures are at their most pleasant.

Green it isn't, but Death Valley is not without its own palette of colours. The canyons and mountains around it see to that. Golden Canyon shines gold and purple; Mustard Canyon is shaded ochre and the Black Mountains sport reds, greens and tans. Mosaic Canyon is so named for the colourful pebbles embedded into grey rock, giving it a mosaic effect. Death Valley information is available from the park superintendent at Death Valley, CA 92328 (714 786 2331).

Joshua Tree National Monument is in Palm Springs and was created in 1935 despite protests from mining companies wishing to utilize the area for their own purposes. As its name indicates, this is the place of the Joshua Tree and that name was given by early settlers who thought it resembled the prophet Joshua with his arms raised.

The Visitor's Center and museum are located at Twentynine Palms Oasis where there is also a short nature trail which will orient you with the park's plant and animal life. Although not all the roads through the 870sq mi (2252sq km) park are good, the main one is. One of the notable landmarks is Split Rock, near Pinto Wye – a giant split boulder with a cave underneath. Don't miss either the Cholla Cactus gardens and nature trail ten miles (16km) away, but do watch out for those stinging jumping cholla cacti – they're painful if they catch you!

Favorite place on the Monument grounds is Wonderland of the Rocks in Hidden Rock. Time and wind have sculpted the rocks here into all kinds of shapes, which with imagination, can seem to be things other than rocks. Park information from the superintendent, 74485 Palm Vista Drive, Twentynine Palms, CA 92277 (714 367 7571).

Muir Woods National Monument is a popular side trip from San Francisco across the Golden Gate Bridge to the Marin Peninsula. The Redwood Creek Nature Trail which runs for a quarter of a mile is cool and tranquil to take of a summer afternoon. The Monument is located on the southwestern slope of Mt. Tamalpais and comprises a representative group of the West Coast's celebrated redwoods.

Merced River, Yosemite

Yosemite Valley

Big: Sequoia, Yosemite

Bigger: El Capitan, Yosemite

Biggest: Grand Canyon

LOS ANGELES

History Los Angeles was founded when Spain renewed its interest in California due to the potential threats from other nations, namely Russia, Britain, and the American colonies themselves (growing steadily powerful in the East). In 1769, it was little more than an Indian village. Gaspar de Portola and Father Crespi gave it the name Pueblo del Rio de Nuestra Senora la Reina de los Angeles – a name that was later abbreviated – and founded the city around Olvera St.

Once Mexico became free from Spain in 1822 and new rulers moved into California, Los Angeles was made the capital for the next decade. But once again power changed hands as the Mexican-American war came and went in 1848, although the city itself had already been taken over a year earlier by Stockton and General Stephen Kearny.

Ranchers in the vicinity prospered greatly by the Gold Rush. So many newcomers had to be fed as they headed West for 'finds' of the precious metal that in the 1850s and early 1860s, just prior to the Civil War, cattle were selling for $400 a head. The new railroads made Los Angeles expand, too. Few people could resist the $1 fares from Mississippi junction to L.A., instituted by the Southern Pacific and Santa Fe rail companies in 1885.

At the end of the Gold Rush era, a number of miners stayed out West but changed their professions to banking, farming, and fishing. By the 1860s, L.A. was already an important banking center, and after the Civil War many homesteaders came to grow oranges. Giant belts of citrus fruit were planted to help meet the demands of the East. While the completion of the transcontinental railroad aided the orchards, oddly enough, Los Angeles was not allowed to join the network until 1876. Even so, by 1872, there were 35,000 orange trees in Los Angeles County and soon they spread throughout the other counties. After 1893, growers formed a marketing organization which paved the way for the founding of the Fruit Growers' Exchange of 1895, which in turn paved the way for the Fruit Growers' Exchange of 1905 which traded under the familiar name 'Sunkist'.

Los Angeles did not really progress rapidly until the turn of the century. San Pedro was selected as the new harbor turning the city into a first class port. In 1909, San Pedro and Wilmington were both encompassed to form an extended harbor district. New port facilities prior to the formal opening of the Panama Canal made Los Angeles a great American harbor city and an important world harbor – greater than San Francisco.

In the first decade of the 20th century, L.A. tripled the size of its population from almost 102.5 thousand in 1900. Petroleum was discovered and this 'black gold' production was booming in the 1920s. the population moved northwards pushing L.A. to reach Beverly Hills, the Hollywood Hills, and San Fernando. To the west it bulged out to meet Culver City and to the south, a large number of 'suburbs'.

The twenties brought cars by the hundred, their dealers taking over all of Figueroa and Alvarado boulevards, causing the demise of the city's trolley system and many trains. The twenties also brought bigger and better banking. A 1929 merger between First National and the Security National Bank put one of America's largest banks in L.A. Also in the twenties fame came to Hollywood as the world's major film center.

At this time, the city was justifiably wearing a metropolitan cloak. It got a civic center at last and a new Union passenger railroad terminal. Streamlined transcontinental trains arrived; a metropolitan water system was constructed; and an observatory built at Griffith Park. In later years, there was a shift from single family homes to high-rise apartments. Skyscrapers soared. Los Angeles had arrived! And neither World War II, nor the black riots of the 1960s in Watts have stopped its growth. It has today become a world trade center and convention city. It may be a city of parking lots but they never stay that way.

Where to stay The best thing to remember about Los Angeles is it is segmented and therefore so are the accommodations, from budget to luxury. Downtown, the most spectacular for size is the

Bonaventure whose gleaming towers have added something new to the city skyline. The giant edifice on Figueroa St boasts 1,500 rooms, an atrium lobby and so many restaurants it's hard to decide where to eat. The Hilton is another mammoth building on Wilshire Blvd, near the entrances of several major freeways. It manages to shut itself off by turning towards a subtropical garden. Another in the deluxe bracket is the Hyatt Regency at Broadway Plaza, which is part and parcel of the adjacent shopping and business complex. With its revolving roof top dining spot and its executive services, it's often a number one choice.

The New Otani next to the Music Center is one of those unique hotels – a Japanese spa that features shiatsu massage as well as the almost obligatory classical Japanese gardens. If you like your setting traditional classic, pick the Biltmore on South Olive St. It's massive, but a grand dame of L.A. hotels where visitors will drop in for a meal or drinks whether or not they're staying there. And if you're into the moderate bracket, downtown motels like the City Center and Downtowner, are reasonable.

No Los Angeles hotel is actually on the perimeter of the airport, but there are several excellent ones in its vicinity, such as the Marriott on West Century Blvd. This hotel is luxury all the way including a free-form pool with a 'swim up' bar. Motels in a lower category are plentiful as well. Marina del Rey (fairly convenient area for the airport and a lively yachting center) has its own quota of hotels. The Marina International on Admiralty Way is top bracket with 25 unique villas among its accommodation choice. The Marina del Rey Hotel has a prime waterfront location so outdoor dining is a plus factor here. Among the recommended motels is the Jolly Roger.

Familiar names to look for in the beach cities are Quality Inn and Holiday Inn but a host of hotels and motels can be found along the South Bay and from Santa Monica to Malibu.

Among the leaders in Hollywood area is the Hollywood Roosevelt on Hollywood Blvd, across the street from Mann's Chinese Theater. Its rooms, all remodelled, include poolside lanais and the setting is a garden. One of the more reasonable places in the area is the Saharan Motor Hotel on Sunset Blvd, which is surrounded by famous clubs and restaurants. There's a Holiday Inn in the district, lots of motels and holiday apartments.

Wilshire Blvd houses several impressive hotels like the Ambassador, which has long been a Los Angeles landmark in its 23

Bonaventure Hotel, Los Angeles

acres of grounds. Well seasoned but even plusher after an expensive facelift, this hotel has its own tennis and health club. At some time or another, it has probably hosted every notable celebrity (besides being the setting for the tragic assassination of Robert Kennedy). The Hyatt Wilshire is another upper bracket hostelry, for anyone who requires push-button comfort and likes modern glass palaces. for more moderate accommodations, look to the Best Western Executive Motor Inn and the Wilshire Dunes Motor Hotel.

L'Ermitage is a luxuriously quiet type of hotel with beautiful suites and free limousine service within Beverly Hills. The Beverly Wilshire has the name that everyone knows, and seems to play host to 'everyone', particularly the silver screen variety. You come here 'to see' and 'be seen', but actually it is neither snobby nor stuffy. The Beverly Hills is much more so as celebrities come here to relax rather than sign autographs. You'll find them, though, in the Polo Lounge. One of the most distinctive hotels in the area is the Westwood Marquis whose suites are all individually decorated. Moderate accommodations include a Holiday Inn, a TraveLodge, a Ramada and the St Regis Motor Hotel.

There are less familiar names in the valleys, but if you want to be close to a film set, there's the Sheraton Universal, which is actually in Universal City. There's an unblocked view from every window since the tower is glass and Universal's own designers and decorators were let loose to do the decor. Another choice for the movie minded is Sportsmen's Lodge at Studio City, decorated in what is referred to as 'English country' style, but also with an American style Olympic-sized pool.

Others to note on Ventura Blvd include the Chalet Lodge, the St George Motor

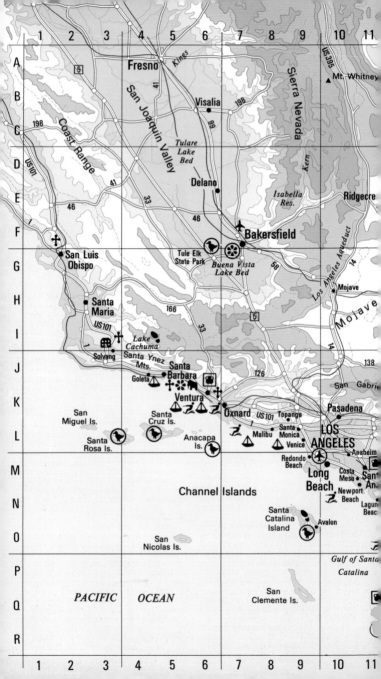

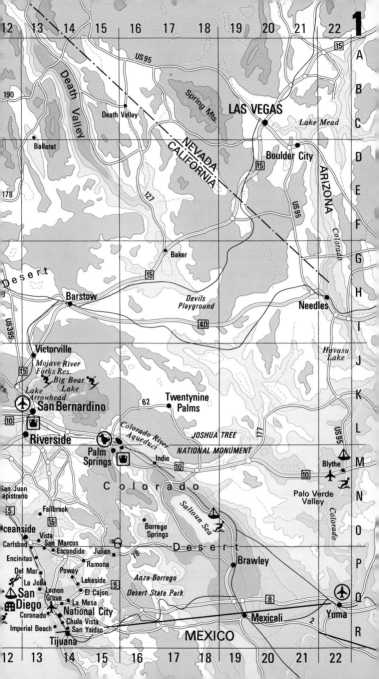

Inn and the Valley Hilton. On Sepulveda Blvd, the Chase House Motel and Royal Oaks Motel are reasonable. In the San Gabriel Valley, there are Holiday Inns, a Hilton and Ramada.

Eating Out The cuisine of every nationality is represented somewhere in Los Angeles with Chinese and Japanese (in their own quarters of town), Mexican, and Hawaiian being especially strong. Currently the following are among the best of downtown restaurants. Francois at Arco Plaza which has won awards for its French menu whose specialities include roast duck and pheasant. Beaudry's in the Bonaventure also offers fine continental cuisine and vintage wines. The oldest steak house in L.A. is the Pacific Dining Car, featuring prime rib cooked over charcoal (on West 6th St). Lawry's California Center offers a Fiesta Dinner in summer with mariachi music and a fixed price for an al fresco meal. Candlelight and a warm friendly atmosphere are part of the charm at O'Shaughnessy's in Arco Plaza with steak and chicken wellington among the specialities. The pricey Pavilion Center in the Music Center has an elegant subdued atmosphere and features great buffets. For inexpensive snacks, sample Vickman's, the oldest downtown gathering place in the produce market. Breakfast is the special occasion here but at lunch and dinner there are hot pies, fresh pastries, and fruits.

In Marina Del Rey, The Warehouse is a recommended choice. Exotic drinks and the catch of the day! All in a dramatic boating setting. There's intimate dining at the Crystal Seahorse in the Marina del Rey Hotel plus award-winning continental cuisine. Don the Beachcomber's is a recognizable name, with a Saturday night luau. There's one on Bali Way and one on the Pacific Coast Highway. T.J. Peppercorn's at the Hyatt near the airport has fresh seafood, duck, a romantic atmosphere, and good desserts and salad bars.

Along the South Bay, look out for Pancho's on Highland Ave where the food's Mexican and the venue, a lush garden. Captain Kidd's Fish Market in Redondo Beach prepares a wide variety of seafood the American way. Casa Maria is a family style Mexican eatery.

In Hollywood, Antonio's on Melrose Ave has a carnival atmosphere about it which Mexican classical dishes and strolling musicians help to create. Yamashiro is a Hollywood landmark on North Sycamore. Great view and Japanese-continental cuisine. Los Feliz Inn at the base of the Griffith Park foothills emphasizes daily specialities in a country inn setting.

One block south of Wilshire Blvd, The Cove has a first class reputation for seafood and prime rib and an olde worlde ambience. The Windsor on West 7th has won many awards for A-1 dining of the classical kind. If you like a clubby atmosphere, this is a winner. Perino's is another first class Wilshire Blvd recommendation.

Italian specialities and often a star studded clientele make La Scala in Beverly Hills a favorite. More Italian at La Famiglia on North Canyon Drive where the pasta is plentiful and good. Well-known theatrical people often gather at the Ginger Man on North Bedford. For something less expensive, try The Cheesecake Factory (30 varieties) or The Magic Pan. Stratton's, by the way, in Westwood, is an unexpected haven with interesting seafood dishes.

Entertainment All the top hotels have some kind of entertainment, but the Los Angeles club scene isn't what it used to be. Hot spots are more likely to be at the beach resorts – discos, folk clubs, jazz clubs etc., but they have been known to close 'overnight'.

Downtown, the Club Mikado on South Figueroa St is a classy hostess club and Restaurant Horikawa on South San Pedro St, is one of those with a piano bar. The Warehouse in Marina del Rey has live entertainment nightly. Many other places in the area have entertainment on weekends and special brunches. At The Body Shop on Sunset Blvd, you can see burlesque dancers and there's gypsy music at Mischa's Restaurant on the same boulevard. At the time of writing,, La Cage aux Folles on La Cienega Blvd, has a great little revue. La Fonda on Wilshire Blvd has one of the best mariachi bands.

One of the places still holding its own is the Troubadour on Santa Monica Blvd, which has in the past booked plenty of star talent. There's jazz at the Baked Potato, rock style – in North Hollywood and sometimes at Mulberry St, a N. Hollywood club, Dante's, too, in the same area. And The Lighthouse at Hermosa Beach offers a variety of jazz entertainers.

Sport The Dodgers baseball team's home stadium is at 1000 Elysian Park Ave. They play there from April to September, but the 56,000-capacity stadium is used for other events the rest of the year. The Pasadena Rose Bowl and the Forum are two more places to watch ball games.

For horse racing, there's Santa Anita Park in Arcadia; or Hollywood Park. Biking is good around Westwood UCLA campus or Griffith Park and fishing or sailing boats are to be rented at Marina del Rey. Watersports are available at all the beach resorts while golf and tennis may be played year round at both public and private clubs throughout Greater Los Angeles.

A Walking Tour of Old Town is perhaps the only real walking tour you can make in L.A. Remember, the city's made for driving! Go first to the Visitors' Center, 100 Paseo de la Plaza from where organized walking tours (free) leave several times a day from Tues.–Sat., and will show you the beginnings of L.A. as a pueblo (a historic landmark since 1781 and since restored). Start at the **Old Plaza**. Opening directly onto it is the **Old Mission Church** dating from 1818 and the city's oldest. Open daily for visiting, it contains paintings and religious relics.

The block-long, pedestrian-zoned **Olvera St** is today a Mexican marketplace with shops and cafes. The merchandize for sale is all authentic Mexican as is the food – the simple cafe kind, or the sit-down, higher priced restaurant variety. Mexican crafts are on show in the Trade Mart and you can watch craftsmen at work on leather, silver, and glass.

On this street is the **Avila Adobe**, the city's oldest adobe building (1818). Open daily, for free, it was built by Don Francisco Avila and has a front veranda plus a flower-filled garden at the back. **Pico House** (named for California's last Mexican governor) is also old (1870) and was the first three-storey building to be constructed as a prestige hotel. This is found on Main St.

In the same district, you will see the **Merced Theatre**, the **Sepulveda House**, and the **Pelanconi House**, one of the first two-storey brick buildings in L.A. After the tour, stroll over to **Union Passenger Terminal**, where the stars of the thirties would alight to the popping of camera flashes, their latest beaux in tow. The terminal, located on North Alameda St is said to be one of the last of its kind to be built in America – a great 50-acre terminal with landscaped patios, arched passageways and fountains.

One of the highlights of the Olvera tour is a look at the tunnels which led from the warehouses to the Pico House. They were first used by the workers using the hotel for lunch without having to take the more dangerous way, across the street, minding the horse traffic. Later, when the Chinese moved in, they became opium and gambling dens.

Other Walking Tours include **Chinatown**, the 900 block of N. Broadway, a typically Oriental sector with shops and groceries specializing in Chinese goods and delicacies, and restaurants serving Cantonese cuisine. **Little Tokyo** features the tea houses, Japanese shops (selling anything, it seems, ever made in Japan), and restaurants. Located at San Pedro and First Sts, it serves as the social, economic, cultural, and religious centre for the largest Japanese-American community in the mainland USA.

A walk up Hollywood Blvd is a must – passing on the way Mann's Chinese Theater and several museums relating to the film industry (See Museums). A guided tour of the **Music Center** (free several times a week throughout the year) is also top priority. It is located in the same complex as the **Civic Center** (a multistorey array of shops and restaurants in a landscaped mall), between Temple and First Sts, one block south of Figueroa. The Center comprises three theaters: The **Mark Taper Forum**, the **Ahmanson Theater** and the **Dorothy Chandler Pavilion** where the opera and orchestra both play.

Music Center, Los Angeles

Beverly Hills also may be walked through as it is a compact municipality. The main thoroughfare is Wilshire but the heart of Beverly Hills is where Beverly, Rodeo, and Camden Drives merge. The majority of tourists will take a bus tour of Beverly Hills in order to view the **Stars' Homes**. The most celebrated of the old houses is Pickfair atop the ridge at Summit Drive, once the home of Mary Pickford. Not all the fancy mansions do indeed belong to the film set. There is one with garish statuary that belongs to a young Arab prince. And there is Greystone Mansion at Lima Vista Drive and Doheny Rd, built in the twenties at huge cost by oil millionaire Edward Doheny.

Other Attractions An organized bus tour will take you to **Farmers Market**, at Fairfax and Third, or you can get there yourself from a downtown base. Originally, back in the Depression years, this was a group of stalls in a field where farmers tried to do business. Now there are many

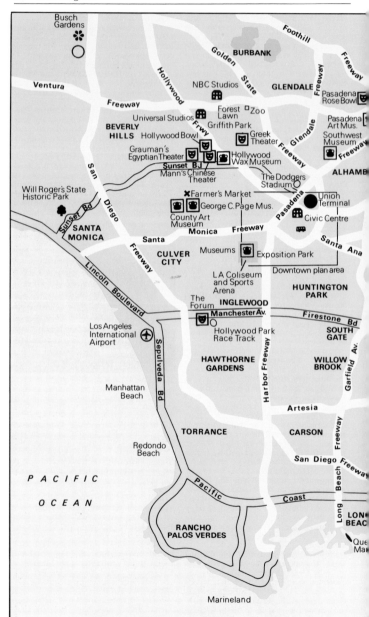

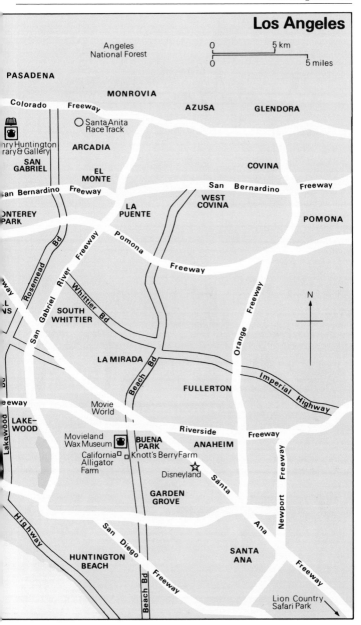

Los Angeles

Angeles National Forest

0   5 km
0   5 miles

PASADENA

MONROVIA

AZUSA   GLENDORA

Colorado   Freeway

○ Santa Anita Race Track

Henry Huntington Library & Gallery

ARCADIA

SAN GABRIEL

COVINA

EL MONTE

San Bernardino   Freeway

San Bernardino Freeway

WEST COVINA

MONTEREY PARK

LA PUENTE

POMONA

Rosemead Bd

San Gabriel River Freeway

Whittier Bd

Pomona

Freeway

SOUTH WHITTIER

Orange Freeway

N

LA MIRADA

Beach Bd

FULLERTON

Imperial Highway

Movie World

Riverside   Freeway

Movieland Wax Museum

BUENA PARK

ANAHEIM

Lakewood

LAKE-WOOD

California Alligator Farm

Knott's Berry Farm

☆ Disneyland

Newport Freeway

GARDEN GROVE

Santa

Ana

Highway

San Diego   Freeway

HUNTINGTON BEACH

Beach Bd

Freeway

SANTA ANA

Freeway

Lion Country Safari Park

Surfing, Malibu

Disneyland, the entrance

Airport building, Los Angeles

Walk of Fame, Los Angeles

Marineland, Los Angeles

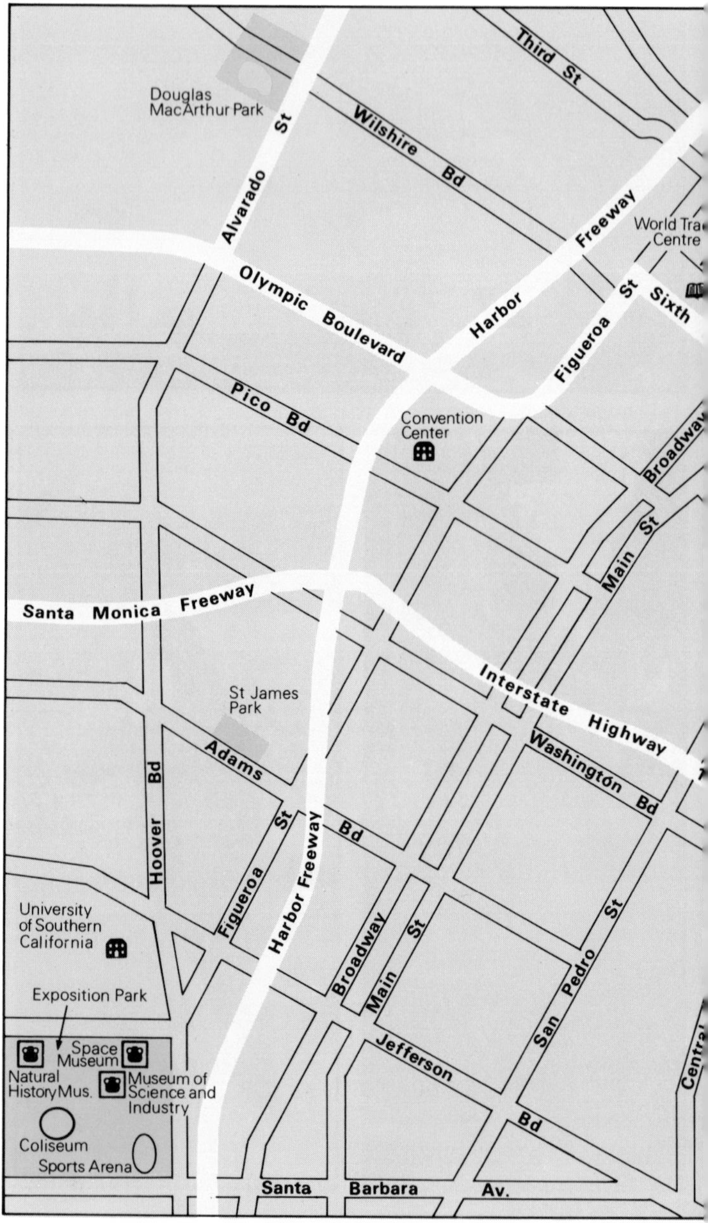

Third St

Douglas
MacArthur Park

Alvarado St

Wilshire Bd

Freeway

World Trade
Centre

Olympic Boulevard

Harbor

Figueroa St

Sixth

Pico Bd

Convention
Center

Broadway

Main St

Santa Monica Freeway

Interstate Highway

St James
Park

Adams

Washington Bd

Hoover Bd

Figueroa St

Harbor Freeway

Bd

Broadway

Main St

San Pedro St

University
of Southern
California

Exposition Park

Space
Museum

Natural
History Mus.

Museum of
Science and
Industry

Jefferson

Coliseum

Sports Arena

Central

Santa   Barbara   Av.

Bd

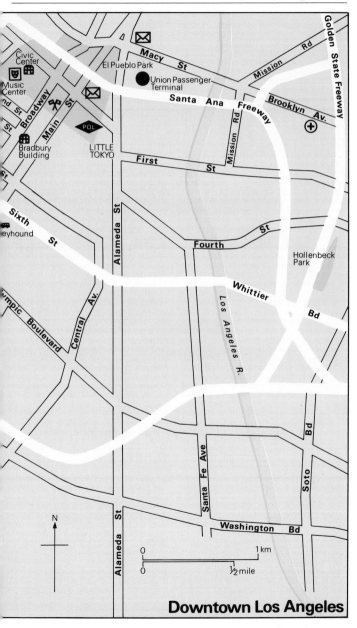

Downtown Los Angeles

more stalls and the structure is a little more permanent. Nor do the farmers have to try quite so hard for business – everyone loves to come here, to buy fresh fruit and veg, sample a host of different foods from takeaway stalls, or in sit-down cafes. There are juice and salad bars, chili kiosks, barbecue pits, fish and oyster bars. And the prices are most reasonable.

An organized bus tour will also take you to the **Toluca** area, home of the studios. Located at the base of the Hollywood Hills, its name stems from two natural, artesian-fed lakes. Basically, it is Hollywood's overflow with a third of the area belonging to **Burbank**, the rest under the umbrella of Los Angeles. From Hollywood, it may be reached via the Cahuenga Pass, Barham Blvd, or Lankershim Blvd. From anywhere else, take the Golden State, Hollywood or Ventura freeways, into the San Fernando Valley.

It is a well-developed area with Verdugo Rd to the north, Buena Vista to the east, Forest Lawn and the Hills to the south, Lankershim Blvd to the west. The big TV and film studios are here, like **Universal** where a tour is more than worthwhile. (See Young West Coast).

From here, it is easy to reach **Forest Lawn** which is situated in Glendale and is that famous cemetery Evelyn Waugh satirized in his book *The Loved One*. The highlight is the Great Mausoleum where a *Last Supper* window, based on Leonardo da Vinci's painting is displayed in the Memorial Court of Honor daily at 1000, 1100 and every half hour from 1200–1600. The window is the work of Rosa Moretti, the last member of an Italian family said to have a secret process for making stained glass. A number of well-known Californians are entombed in this mausoleum, including Jean Harlow and Clark Gable.

Next to the Forest Lawn Museum (which has a reproduction of Gilberti's **Paradise Doors**), there is a special theater which shows two paintings when the single curtain, 210ft (64m) long and 65ft (20m) high, is drawn. *The Crucifixion* is the largest permanently mounted painting in America, painted by Jan Styka. The other painting displayed is *The Resurrection* by Robert Clark. They are on view every half hour from 1100–1700.

Another attraction is the Court of David where there is a reproduction of Michelangelo's celebrated statue. (Stuatuary is scattered throughout Forest Lawn, reproductions of famous pieces and otherwise.) There are also several interesting churches, like the Church of the Recessional, modelled after a 10th century English one. In the adjoining wing, Rudyard Kipling's family album

and literary mementoes are on view. Similarly, Wee Kirk o' the Heather is patterned after a 14th century Scottish church and one of its stained glass windows depicts the story of Annie Laurie.

Griffith Park at Los Feliz Blvd and Vermont Ave is one of Los Angelenos' favorite recreational areas with over 4,000 acres. The natural mountainside greenery provides a pleasant place for picnicking, sports, and there are several attractions worth visiting within the park. The nearest entrance to Hollywood is at the northern end of Western Blvd. A second entrance can be found at the northern tip of Vermont Ave (leading to the Greek Theater, Observatory, bird sanctuary, and Mount Hollywood). The entrance at the junction of Los Feliz Blvd and Riverside Dr leads to the golf course and zoo. And there's a fourth entrance at Ventura and Golden State Freeways.

Throughout the summer, there are first class performances at the **Greek Theater**, one of L.A.'s best known amphitheaters. The **Los Angeles Zoo** is popular for family outings. More than 50 species in danger of extinction are housed in the 80-acre zoo, which is divided into continental areas and contains altogether more than 2,000 animals from around the world. See also the special children's section. Open in summer daily 1000–1800 and in winter, 1000–1700.

On top of Mt Hollywood is the **Planetarium** on Vermont Ave housed in the **Griffith Observatory**. 'A trip to the moon', or Jupiter or Saturn, a look at the Northern Lights – are all possible in the 500-seat theater and there's a Hall of Science and twin refracting telescope here too. A laserium show is featured twice daily. Open in summer 1300–2200 Sun.–Fri.; 1130–2200 Sat. In winter: 1400–2200 Tues.-Fri.; 1130–2200 Sat.

Ferndell is one of the prettiest sections of the park planted with ferns from all over the globe, and an ideal picnic place. **Travel Town** is for the kids who can clamber at will over old rail cars, and not far away they can take a ride on a miniature train, or a pony if preferred – near Los Feliz and Riverside Drive.

Hancock Park on Curson Ave at Wilshire Blvd is mainly the home of art and anthropological museums. (See Museums.) **Hollywood Memorial Park** on Santa Monica Blvd is the last resting place for people like Peter Lorre and Tyrone Power. The **Hollywood Bowl** is on sightseeing itineraries because the building is so impressive – it holds thousands. This is the summer home of the Philharmonic Orchestra whose season runs July to September.

Despite its office crammed centers, Los Angeles does lay claim to several gardens and parks where peace reigns. Some have already been mentioned. Some are listed in Young West Coast. Among the others, visit: the **Arboretum** on N. Baldwin Ave in Arcadia where the world's plants are gathered on a 27-acre estate. Begonias and orchids are the special feature along with demonstration home gardens and shopping and eating facilities are on the premises. Open daily 0900–1630.

Descanso Gardens on Descanso Drive are famous for their camellias – 100,000 of them in an oak-forest setting. Rose gardens are the other feature and there is a Japanese tea house as well as picnic facilities. Open daily 0900–1630. **Rose Hills Memorial Park** on S. Workman Mill Rd., Whittier, is home of the Pageant of Roses Garden, a 2,650 acre area that includes its own Japanese garden. Open daily 0800 to dusk. **South Coast Botanic garden** on Grenshaw Blvd, Palos Verdes Peninsula shows off Californian native plants and trees to advantage in an 87-acre area with a man-made lake. Open daily 0900–1630.

Olvera St is Los Angeles' oldest quarter, but with time to spare in the metropolis, there are some other small quarters to be seen. The **Bradbury Building** (1813) on S. Broadway, for example, has so much wrought iron and marble, ornate lifts and other Victorian touches, that it is often used as a 'set' for movies. The 1300 block of **Carrol Ave** between E. Edgeware Rd and Douglas, has the highest concentration of Victorian residences. **Heritage Square** on Homer St is now a park site containing Victorian structures brought here from other neighborhoods and restored. **Grand Central Public Market** has been a downtown L.A. landmark since 1917 and is a gathering place these days for those in the know, out to eat cheaply or buy fresh produce.

McArthur Park, Los Angeles

Anaheim M11

Part of Orange County and reached from L.A. via the Santa Ana Freeway and best known for its host of family attractions like Disneyland and Knotts Berry Farm (see Young West Coast). Next door to Disneyland is the Anaheim Convention Center which not only caters to business groups, but is equally the site of concerts, sporting events, circuses, and ice shows. An impressive complex spread over 40 acres, it will be one of the world's largest and most versatile when its extension is completed some time in 1983.

Anaheim's stadium on College Blvd cost $21 million to build but it is the local home of the California Angels baseball team and their fans think it's worth it. It seats 44,000 for a baseball game and up to 56,000 watching the other sports events held here.

Shopping facilities are bar none either modern multi-storey centers, or 'villagey' complexes. At the Anaheim Plaza, for instance, there are 70 shops, boutiques, and services and a bus link with eight hotel/motels. At the Brookside Vineyards, wine related gifts may be purchased and there are daily tastings at the Winery, open seven days a week 1000–1800.

Finding a place to stay poses no problem since there are currently more than 150 hotels and motels in the area, including TraveLodges, Holiday Inns, a Hyatt, Howard Johnsons, Inn on the Park and a variety of not so familiar names, in all price ranges. Disneyland's 'official hotel' (Disneyland Hotel) is an Anaheim resort in itself and on the monorail system.

Eating also poses no problem – from take-out to gourmet, it's to be found in Anaheim's restaurants and hotels. The Area Visitor and Convention Bureau publishes a dining guide describing location and facilities.

All sports are available including golf at the Anaheim Hills Public Country Club (an 18-hole course in the Santa Ana canyons) and at the Anaheim Municipal Golf Course where there is daily play (18 holes) from dawn to dusk. One of the top tennis facilities is the Tennisland Racquet Club (a block from Disneyland). Although a private club, it is available to guests of major hotels in the area and most of the courts are night lit.

Buena Park, Anaheim, boasts six major attractions: Knott's Berry Farm, Enchanted Village, Alligator Farm, Movieland Wax Museum, Movieworld (see Young West Coast) and the Palace of Living Art. The latter is adjacent to the Wax Museum and its highlights include a ten-ton marble reproduction of Michelangelo's *David* as well as a Carrara marble copy of his *Pieta*.

Reproductions of over 40 statues, the originals of which are found in the Louvre, are also on display. And famous paintings like the *Mona Lisa* have been duplicated in detail.

Tours are given of the Crystal Cathedral which is a new landmark for Southern California, designed by Philip Johnson. From a distance it simulates a giant glass obelisk and from the air it resembles a four-pointed star. 12,000 panes of glass were used in its construction and there are no pillars to obstruct one's view. The chancel area is made from Spanish Rosso Alicante marble; the pulpit and communion table are granite. The organ is a combination of the Aeolian Skinner from Lincoln Center and the Garden Grove Community Church Fratelli-Ruffatti comprised of more than 13,000 pipes. It's located at the corner of Chapman and Lewis Sts in Garden Grove and tours are generally given 0900–1600 Mon.–Sat. and Sun. 1230–1630.

There's a full range of nightlife from the usual to the unusual. The Cowboy, for example, may have you thinking you're in Texas, not California at all. It's one of Orange County's largest and most popular clubs, featuring country music, a mechanical bucking bull and dances like the Texas Twostep. Sebastian's at the Grand is a dinner playhouse, one of several in the area. A buffet precedes a musical revue with dessert offered at intermission.

If you want to know what's happening in Anaheim and the Orange County, ring the guest information number (635 8900).

Bakersfield   F7
Gateway to national parks and the high Sierras. These days an agricultural and music centre, it used to be a rough tough town in the Gold Rush days. It wears two titles: 'Capital of the Golden Empire' and 'Nashville of the West'. (There are several professional country and western recording studios located here.) Accommodations include a TraveLodge, Best Western, and Vagabond. Holiday areas have been developed in and around Bakersfield with boating, fishing, and swimming possible in the reservoirs.

Visit nearby Pioneer Village, a museum with 35 original or restored historic buildings and a collection of Indian relics and fossils. South of Bakersfield is fort Tejon, a reconstruction of the military base which was active here between 1854 and 1964.

West of town is Tule Elk State Park where one of the world's rarest animals is kept on a 965-acre reserve. Visitors can go into the viewing area to see the elk, but the range itself is closed to the public. Best viewing time is around feeding time, 1400.

For watersports, visit Buena Vista Aquatic Recreation Area, a 1,586 acre playground where there are two lakes, picnic and camping grounds, boating, fishing, and swimming facilities. This lies to the south of town. Another favorite area is located to the north and east – Kern River Valley. This region offers some of California's finest horseback riding, water and snow skiing, camping, boating, golf, kayaking, hunting, and swimming. Fishing is possible in the Kern River's pools. At the headwaters of the river is manmade Lake Isabella with a 38mi (60km) shoreline. Modern motels and lodges, a golf course, and many watersports are to be found around the lake.

Big Bear Lake   K14
It is Southern California's largest lake and mountain resort 7000ft (2133m) above sea level in a pine setting. The seven mile (11km) long lake is well stocked with trout and fishing here is allowed year round, without a license. Horseback riding, hunting, and camping can be enjoyed in Big Bear Lake Valley. In winter, there are opportunities for skiing, snowmobiling, tobogganing, and ice skating.

Every October, there's an Oktoberfest bringing Germany's carnival atmosphere to this alpine setting. Bavarian folk dances, beer, and bands plus German food make it almost like Munich.

A two-hour drive from Los Angeles, beyond San Bernardino, on State 18.

Blythe   M22
Blythe and the Palo Verde Valley offer many sporting activities including boating, fishing, and water skiing. The area near the town is famous for semi-precious stones like agate and quartz and there are several old mines in the vicinity. North of Blythe visitors may see 500-year-old Indian pictographs. Hunting is possible near Palo Verde, for geese, quail, duck, and dove. There is an 18-hole championship golf course overlooking the Palo Verde Valley which proves a real challenge.

Blythe is 200mi (321km) east of Los Angeles on Interstate 10.

Borrego Springs   P16
A desert oasis in the vicinity of San Diego with an average year-round temperature in the 70s. Summer months can rise to over 100°. Motels, including luxury ones, are plentiful, and include La Casa del Zorro. Sports facilities include golf, tennis, and swimming pools. Best known for its surrounding park, the Anza-

Borrego Desert State Park (see Parks).

Ninety miles (145km) northeast of San Diego off State 78. The best route is east on Interstate 8 to Descanso, north on State 79 to Julian, east on 78.

Carlsbad   P13

A beachside community within easy access of San Diego, which was named for Karlsbad, Bohemia, the famed European spa. At one time, the city had an artesian well, but today it no longer produces water. Instead, it is a historical site marked by a gazebo in the Alt Karlsbad complex.

Watersports are the key to this resort. Swimming and surfing are available in two state parks; Carlsbad State Beach and South Carlsbad State Beach (where there is a large campsite). Sailing, waterskiing, and fishing are favored at Agua Hedionda Lagoon while the Buena Vista Lagoon is a bird sanctuary for 125 species of migratory waterfowl.

Carlsbad has several motels including a Best Western, but the time honored resort is La Costa which specializes in golf and tennis facilities.

Thirty-five miles (56km) north of San Diego on Interstate 5.

Catalina Island   08

A pretty, cove-fringed island 26mi (41km) off the California coast, ideal for the family. It began as a resort when it was bought by William Wrigley (of chewing gum fame) in 1919 and is noted today for its flying fish, porpoises, and undersea gardens.

The island's capital, Avalon, has a pleasure pier which is departure point for glass-bottom and flying fish boats. (A combination tour ticket is sold which includes a glass-bottom boat trip plus a ride to watch the sea colony along the eastern tip of the island.)

Novelist Zane Grey spent his last 20 years living on this island and his home is now a comfortable guest house – the Zane Grey Pueblo Hotel. Hiking, fishing, swimming, and cycling are among the available sporting activities. Daily cruises to the island depart from Long Beach, Newport Beach, and San Pedro and Catalina Air makes regular trips (15 minutes).

Chula Vista   R14

Basically a farming community, this town is midway between San Diego and Tijuana and this puts it on the mainstream. It has a large shopping district, many excellent restaurants and lots of places to stay including a Best Western, a Ramada, and the Vagabond Motor Hotel.

Its name comes from the Spanish for 'beautiful view' which is a natural for its setting, between mountains and sea.

Coronado   R14

An island right in San Diego Bay and connected to downtown by a long narrow sandbar known as the Silver Strand. Before 1969, it could only be reached by ferry or a drive via Imperial Beach to the south. Nowadays a bridge offers the easiest way to reach it. Coronado, known as the 'Crown City', is most famous for its Hotel Del Coronado which has been visited by at least eight presidents. The historic landmark was completed in 1888, adjacent to the North Island Naval Air Station from where Charles Lindbergh set off on the first leg of his flight to Paris in 1927.

Costa Mesa   M11

A university and residential community adjoining Newport Beach, but located in Orange County, on the San Diego Freeway 40mi (64km) south of Los Angeles. One of its features is the **Briggs Cunningham Automotive Museum** on East Baker St which houses a considerable collection of automobiles in its 30,000 sq ft (2,800 sq m) exhibition hall, dating from 1898 to present times. Such vintage cars as a 1927 super deluxe Bugatti 'Royale' sports car are on view, Open Wed.–Sun. 0900–1700.

All of Newport Beach's facilities are close by including several good restaurants right at the edge of Costa Mesa, like Harry's Bar & Grill on Martingale Way and Blackbeard's Galley & Grog on the same road.

Del Mar   Q13

A seaside resort where they say 'the surf meets the turf', for there is thoroughbred racing at the Del Mar track from late July to mid September. It is also the site of the annual San Diego Fair – a 14-day event on the 313-acre Exposition Grounds. After the height of summer, it returns to its lazy, sleepy self. Good white beaches and fishing. Accommodations include the Del Mar Inn, Winners Circle Lodge and Tennis Club and Namara Inn.

On the coast 20mi (32km) north of San Diego.

El Cajon   Q14

A good holiday base between the mountains and the sea, this is the hub of San Diego's east county, and includes Bostonia within its city limits (one of the county's oldest communities). It offers plenty of sports facilities and accommodations like a Best Western motel and Pennylodge Motel. The annual Mother

Goose Parade takes place each year here the Sunday before Thanksgiving, a 90-minute spectacle that first started in 1947.

The East County Performing Arts Center is located in the center of El Cajon, hosting major symphony, ballet, and other musical and theatrical performances. Every year, there is a spectacular air show at Gillespie Field.

It is 16mi (25km) east of San Diego on Interstate 8.

Encinitas   P13
A coastal community that is often referred to as 'Flower Capital of the World'. It may not be quite that but it does produce roses, daisies, and chrysanthemums in abundance. Just prior to Christmas the whole area is carpeted in poinsettias and one of the leading growers of this flower is located in Encinitas.

Escondido   P14
A city to be passed on the way to Mt. Palomar. Its surrounding orchards lend it a countrified atmosphere but the city itself is a modern one with theaters, shops, and recreational facilities throughout the valley. There are 17 golf courses within a 20mi (32km) radius. At Dixon Lake, in the hills just above, there are opportunities to fish, picnic, and camp. (There are several campsites scattered through the hills, all with lovely views of the north country.) A variety of accommodation includes the Circle R Golf Resort, Escondido Motor Hotel, and Lawrence Welk Village Inn. The San Diego Wild Animal Park is six miles (9km) away.

On Interstate 15, 29mi (47km) north of San Diego.

Fallbrook   O13
Calls itself the 'Avocado Capital of the World' as well as 'the Friendly Village'. It is friendly in a mid-western sort of way, and it does produce a lot of avocadoes. Since it has always been somewhat off the beaten track, there is little Spanish influence. Accommodations include the Pala Mesa Resort and Fallbrook is gradually gaining importance for antique collectors.

It is off Interstate 15, 45mi (72km) north of San Diego.

Goleta   J4
A holiday weekend getaway just north of Santa Barbara with the Santa Ynez Mountains for a backdrop. At the shaded Pacific beaches one can swim, surf, sportfish, and sail. Goleta can also boast cultural activities that a larger city would be proud to claim.

Attractions in town include a 50-acre

botanic garden, a children's zoo, and sealarium and restored early Californian homes. Of especial interest are the orchid ranches. Within easy driving distance are three missions: Santa Barbara, La Purisima Concepción and Santa Ines (see Missions).

Nearby is Southern California's largest man-made freshwater lake – Lake Cachuma, a popular recreational area with first class tennis and golf facilities, boating and fishing. In the vicinity are hiking trails and campsites.

Imperial Beach   R13
The most southwesterly city in the continental USA, it is mainly quiet and residential despite its claimed title of 'Helicopter Capital of the World'. The reason for the title is that this is a training base for the Pacific Fleet helicopter squadrons.

South of Imperial Beach is the Border Field State Park featuring both a wildlife preserve and beach which may be ridden on. There are horseback trails in the park.

Indio   M17
A year-round holiday city in the Palm Springs-Coachella Valley, surrounded by mountains. Resort fashions are a good buy here in the malls and shopping centers. A host of golf courses are within a ten-minute drive of town including the famous Bob Hope Classic course and three championship public courses. Lots of tennis courts too, mostly night-lit.

Lake Cahuilla, well stocked with fish, is on Indio's doorstep, but it is the date palms which have made the town famous, lending it the title 'Date Capital of the World'.

Julian   P15
A farming center which used to be an old mining town in the boom year of 1870 when gold was struck. Visitors may relive the gold mining experience here by touring the abandoned Eagle and Highpeak Mines.

Along the main road, fruit locally grown is for sale. Beyond the town are cattle pastures and the area is particularly scenic in autumn while in spring, innumerable wildflowers colour the mountains and valleys. A wildflower show is held here annually in spring; a weed show (believe it or not) in late summer; and a harvest festival in the autumn.

Situated at the junction of State 78 and 79, 60mi (96km) north east of San Diego.

Laguna Beach   N11
A much loved centre for painters and artists in a palm and eucalyptus tree

La Jolla

setting. It is a colourful but leisurely colony with boutiques, galleries, small theaters, and coffee houses. The variety of places to stay include the intimate Eiler's Inn and Vacation Village, which has a small private beach. Lots of atmospheric places to eat.

La Jolla   Q13

'The Jewel' as the Spanish would say, though it is pronounced like the Jewish dance. In 1900, this little seaside village was a popular picnic spot for those who took the train from the centre of San Diego. Its picturesque quality inspired artists to paint and write. Today, the train is no more but it's an easy 15 minutes drive from downtown to enjoy its Mediterranean atmosphere.

Its name really evolves from the caves hewn by churning surf – 'la hoya' being the Indian word for cave. There is a winding clifftop walk high on the bluffs overlooking La Jolla Cove from where you can see the caves. The largest of the original seven caves is Sunny Jim Cave, reached via 133 steps and an entrance through the Cave Curiosity Shop at the north end of the Coast Boulevard.

La Jolla Cove is one of the best swimming beaches and also a favourite with skin divers. It is part of the San Diego-La Jolla Underwater Park but to explore it

you must be an experienced diver. The park contains an ecological reserve to protect native flora and fauna. At low tide, the tidepools just beyond Alligator Head at the Cove, are full of hermit crabs.

In the winter, Whale Point is an excellent spot to visit for a glimpse of the giant migrating whales. To reach it, follow the shore south from Alligator Head. Opposite the only large building on the beach is a small cove known as Seal Rock from which you can see another cove – Whale Point.

La Jolla is also a scientific research center, being the site of the University of California at San Diego, the Salk Institute for Biological Studies and the Scripps Institute of Oceanography.

It has its own Museum of Contemporary Art in a dramatic beach setting between Seal Rock and Whale Point. Inside there are paintings and sculpture from around the world. The town itself is very atmospheric with pricey boutiques, pavement cafes, cosy bars, and some first class restaurants like Alfonso's, specializing in Mexican dishes. Many visitors prefer to stay in La Jolla rather than San Diego itself at inns such as the Colonial, The Inn, the Royal, or La Jolla Palms. There are also Best Western and Trave-Lodge motels.

Slightly north of La Jolla is Torrey

Pines State Park, overlooking the sea, where over 1,000 acres protect the region's plants and wildlife. The climate agrees with the Torrey Pine which proliferates in the area and the Torrey Pines Inn (home of the Andy Williams Golf Tourney) is a top place to stay.

Lake Arrowhead K13

A man-made lake located in a mountain setting, providing a year-round recreational area. It is considered to be one of the most unspoilt mountain resorts in Southern California. The lake itself has 14mi (21km) of shoreline and in summer, boating is the key sport – sailing, powerboating, canoeing, with water skiing and fishing. On shore, visitors can ride, hike, play tennis, or golf. In winter, there is skiing here – novices can attend the local ski school for instruction. Lake Arrowhead Village, built in an Alpine style has plenty of shops, restaurants, and motels.

It is situated 9mi (15km) north east of San Bernardino on State 18.

Lakeside Q14

It was named for the beautiful Lindo Lake in 1886. Today, the lake is only a pond but the town, built around it, has grown. It is the gateway to three other pleasure lakes: San Vincente Reservoir, El Capitan Reservoir and Lake Jennings. Lindo Lake Park itself is a pleasant picnic spot.

Lakeside is 21mi (34km) north east of San Diego on State 67.

La Mesa Q14

A residential community just east of San Diego. Winding roads lead to almost hidden private residences and there are large amounts of colorful foliage. Noted for its dark hills, geologists believe them to be made up from some of the oldest volcanic rock in the San Diego area. Every Easter Sunday, a sunrise service is held atop Mt Helix (where a white cross stands) in its amphitheater. Accommodations include La Mesa Hitching Post and La Mesa Lodge.

Lemon Grove Q14

One of Southern California's most rapidly growing suburban areas, Lemon Grove is very rural although shopping facilities are plentiful, and all the attractions of San Diego are nearby. At its height – 450ft (137m) above sea level, between the Pacific and desert, outdoor activities are a joy year-round. Flourishing avocadoes and lemons prove this is a frost-free region.

Long Beach M10

Here you have both the beach and the oil derricks – plus the Queen Mary (see

Ports o' Call Village, near Long Beach

Young West Coast). There is also an entertainment center with a 14,000-seater arena where circuses, ice shows, basketball, and rock concerts are held. Special concerts, plays, and musicals are staged in two theaters here.

There are harbor tours departing from Pierpoint Landing several times a day and an imported London double-decker does an hour-long Sea Lane Harbor tour.

Twenty miles (32km) south of Los Angeles on San Pedro Bay.

Malibu L8

A sparkling beach resort within Greater Los Angeles. In 1857 when it was another sprawling rancho, a far sighted Irishman bought it for 10¢ an acre, although it was a Massachusetts man who saw its potential as an 'American Riviera'. It was the stars, however, who helped realize that dream for when property was leased to Anna Nilsson in 1927, others of the era (John Gilbert, Clara Bow etc.) followed and built homes for themselves there.

Malibu

Malibu is the strip along the West Pacific Coast Highway from the city to the border of Ventura County, at its widest three miles (5km) and at its narrowest, one mile (1.5km). Its wide sandy beaches are good for all watersports – and grunion hunting. A string of motels and restaurants flank the coastal road, such as the Polynesian-style Tonga Lei and hacienda-style Casa Malibu (to stay) and Alice's and The Country Wine Cellar, both pretty and informal (to eat) – all located on the Pacific Highway.

Boating is a popular activity and half day or full day sport fishing trips may be booked. Fishing is possible off the pier at Paradise Cove, four miles (6km) west of Malibu Rd.

Situated 25mi (40km) from Los Angeles on State 1.

National City   Q14
At the hub of San Diego's industrial activity. It has a modern seaport, shopping centers, recreational facilities, and residential sections too. In the five city-owned parks in National City, there are tennis courts, an Olympic-sized pool, children's zoo, a municipal golf course, a fishing pier and boat launching pads. It has its own theater and a museum featuring a good 'Americana' collection. An annual spring event is the Maytime Band Review when junior high and high school bands compete.

Newport Beach   M11
A beach resort that attracts the students who surf, dune-buggy, and hunt grunion here. It is located on a sandy beach strip. Sheltered in the bay between the sand bar and the mainland are Balboa Island and Lido Isle. A ferry departs for Balboa Island from the Newport beach pier (the gathering place). Near the ferry landing, at Fun Zone Dock, boats leave on harbor cruises – daily in summer and only on weekends in winter. Some of the waterfront homes you'll pass along the way belong to film and TV stars.

There are all kinds of accommodations from the familiar Sheraton and Marriott to a number of beach bungalows and holiday apartments for rent. Eating places also run the gamut, from those which are inexpensive, catering to the collegiate crowd, to those which are more expensive like Bob Burns at Fashion Island. Nearby El Roberto specializes in fast food, Mexican-style.

The Balboa Pavilion with its distinctive cupola is the area's landmark. In the early 1900s it was a fashionable spot for beauty contests. Now, fishermen, sightseers, and those out to eat form its clientele.

You can overnight on Balboa Island, too, perhaps at the Balboa Inn which has

seen stars like Jean Harlow and Errol Flynn as guests in the thirties and forties.

On Ocean Ave 35mi (56km) south of Los Angeles.

Oceanside   O13
A pretty and active tourist hub on the Pacific Ocean. Its municipal pier – the longest in the West – extends for over a quarter of a mile (800m). Trams run to the end and no license is needed for fishing. The white sand beaches are lovely – miles of them overlooked by palm trees. Accommodations include Best Western's Royal Scot. Central point for sportfish boats is the Small Craft Harbor where several types of boats may be chartered or rented.

On Interstate 5, 40mi (64km) north of San Diego.

Oxnard   K7
A seaside city offering a host of watersports. Boating and sportfishing enthusiasts should head for Channel Island Harbor where there are marine services, restaurants, and accommodations, like the Hilton Inn, Vagabond Motor Hotel, and Casa Sirena Marina Hotel.

On the western city limits is McGrath State Beach, 300 acres with 175 developed campsites. Other beach areas include Silverstrand, Hollywood-by-the-sea and Point Mugu State Beach.

Oxnard is the gateway to the offshore Channel Islands. Beautiful untrampled beaches, unique vegetation, and large numbers of sea lions are what you'll find. Fishing for salmon, halibut, marlin etc, is good and diving is equally rewarding. Visitors will land at Frenchy's Cove on Anacapa and can take a ranger-guided tour. Charter boats also operate to the other islands noted for the variety of marine and birdlife.

Palm Springs   M15
History It was the Cahuilla Indians who first found the magic of the 'springs' although it was their descendants and the Spanish settlers of 1774 who bestowed the name Agua Caliente on the desert oasis (hot springs). Not much happened before a US government party arrived in 1853, that led to it becoming a regular stage coach stop on the run between Prescott in Arizona and Los Angeles.

In 1876, the Southern Pacific Railroad tracks were laid near to the town but even so it wasn't until 1913 that the healthy climate and pleasant surroundings began attracting visitors in any numbers. Its first school house was built in 1915 and by 1938, it had expanded enough to obtain a charter as a city. Since then it has never looked back.

During the Second World War, the adjacent region was used as a desert combat training centre, but its real gain has been as a resort. Those who originally came for a winter break in nice weather, settled and bought land. Suddenly the desert bloomed with hotels, offices, shopping malls, and apartments.

Nevertheless, despite what some think, the Indians are still the major owner of Palm Springs land – and it's prime property. Their 32,000 acre reservation is located within the city limits while other sections take in the desert and the slopes of San Jacinto Mountains.

Accommodations Most of the hotels and motels are the resort variety with sports amenities, although Palm Springs is also a major convention centre. Trave-Lodge and Ramada both have establishments here but most of the names are not of the familiar chain kind. Almost all of them have a swimming pool and often, a therapeutic pool besides. Prices reach their peak during the glamorous winter season between December and April, but this is also the time when top names perform in hotel lounges.

The Canyon Hotel Racquet and Golf Resort on Palm Canyon Drive is one of the best with its own 18-hole golf course and plenty of tennis courts. Almost as popular is Gene Autry's Hotel. Serious tennis afficionadoes are likely to choose the Tennis Club Hotel on Baristo Rd. The most famous hostelry of all is the Spa, a streamlined complex that includes the Bath House where mineral and steam baths, massage and facials, gym, and pools are all available. it was on this site (Indian Ave) that the Indians gathered for many years.

Eating Out Palm Springs residents like a good barbecue but since the restaurant clientele is a star-spangled one, you can expect a variety of cuisine served in a variety of settings from the gimmicky to somewhere very stylish.

Pal Joeys on Saturnino Rd features those barbecue dinners and is a regular showbiz haunt. Di Amico's on South Palm Canyon Dr is a popular steak house decorated in early Californian fashion. Edwards Mansion was converted from a Victorian mansion to a restaurant in 1978 and is surrounded by its own lovely estate. Josephina's on South Indian Ave is also Victorian, but the specialities are Italian.

Palm Springs' 'Restaurant Row' (featuring a wide range of dining spots) is located on Highway 111 in Rancho Mirage, between Cathedral City and Palm Desert.

Entertainment Palm Springs glitters after dark. Expect the stars to appear at the top hotels during the winter season and since many have homes in the town, you may see them anyway. Most hotels have music for dancing or disco; some have cabaret; and some, piano bars.

Culturally, Palm Springs is also well provided with its own Opera Guild, and events are scheduled all year round by the Community Concerts Associations. Palm Springs Center Theater of the Performing Arts stages professional theater productions.

Sport Golf is *the* sport in Palm Springs, host to many tournaments. There are public and private courses. Of the former, the Municipal 18-hole course is one of the most scenic. The best public tennis complex is the Palm Springs Tennis Center where nine courts are night lit.

Biking and hiking and horseback riding are all readily available to the visitors. Palm Springs marks 14mi (22km) of special routes for biking and some of the trails may just as well be used for hiking or riding. And desert or no desert, even fishing and watersports are possible if you travel a little way out of the city. The Salton Sea, 47mi (75km) from palm Springs, occupies the old Salton Sink which was at one time part of the Gulf of California. It is 38mi (60km) long and may be skied or fished.

Attractions First on the list is a ride up the **Aerial Tramway** which was opened in 1963. At that time it was said to be the world's largest, double-reversible passenger tramway. It takes less than 18 minutes to travel by cable car from Valley Station in Chino Canyon to Mountain Station, which is over 8000ft (2400m) up. And at the top is a restaurant, a panoramic view and skiing in winter. Special events are often held at the tramway's peak.

Moorten Botanical Gardens is the place to go to purchase a cactus, but in any case there are over 2,000 varieties on display in the nursery. Open 0900–1700. The **Palm Springs Desert Museum** contains dioramas showing the desert habitat. More desert (that's what it's all about here) at the **Living Desert Reserve**, a 360-acre piece of pure Colorado Desert where there are outdoor displays and $3\frac{1}{2}$ miles of self-guided nature trails. **Big Morongo Wildlife Reserve/Covington Park** is a regional park used for hiking, picnicking, or studying the desert's wildlife. There are 300 species of native plants growing here.

Indian Canyons belongs to the Agua Caliente Band of Calhuilla Indians. There are many beauty spots here and a number of them have been used for filming. Palm Canyon is the most photographed. Rocky gorges and canyons extend for 15mi

(24km) though an easy footpath leads down into the canyon itself. Riders will take the trail to Andreas Canyon, passing Washingtonia palm trees and element-weathered rock formations. Cliffs act as towering canyon walls and in the stream there are still the grinding mills used by Indians years ago. To the south, Murray Canyon has a good trail leading into it. The easiest canyon to reach from the city is Tahquitz. A foot trail up the canyon stream, starting within the city limits, goes for two miles (3km) before it reaches the Tahquitz Falls, cascading in a 60ft (18m) drop. Anyone preferring to ride to the Falls can use the South Palm Canyon Drive to get there.

Although much of the surrounds may be explored at leisure, there are organized desert expeditions for those who are more adventuresome and wish to learn as much as possible about this part of the state.

Pasadena K11

A residential city in the foothills of the Sierra Madres, in the San Gabriel Valley, where there is an abundance of large estates. It is best known for the Rose Bowl where the New Year's football game between the winners of the East and West leagues is a tradition. The annual Tournament of Roses parade which precedes the football game is also a huge attraction and has been since its beginnings in 1890.

Poway P14

Quiet and rural but a fast growing community, Poway Valley used to be the home of the San Diegueno and Luiseno Indians. In remembrance of the old days, there is an annual Pow Wow Days event, but everything else – shops, schools, houses – is new.

Off Insterstate 5, 20mi (32km) north of San Diego.

Ramona P14

A rural community located in the centre of San Diego County. A good base for horse riding and other outdoor activities although Ramona's biggest business is in poultry. The San Vicente Resort and Conference Center which has its own riding stables, is one of the best places to stay.

Thirty-eight miles (60km) from San Diego on State 67.

Redondo Beach M9

An oceanside resort just north of Palos Verdes on the Pacific Coast Highway which was established by railroad tycoon, Henry Huntington. Although it has become industrial, it remains a modest beach resort and one good for fishing.

Accommodations include the Portofino Inn on Portofino Way and restaurants are plentiful, both at the Redondo Beach Pier and elsewhere.

On the lower level of the pier there are often jazz performances in the concert hall as well as at The Lighthouse, L.A.'s oldest jazz club. Nightlife can be quite lively as can restaurants such as Beachbum Burt's on North Harbor Drive, and the Red Onion.

Ridgecrest E11

Situated in the Indian Wells Valley of the Upper Mojave Desert. The town and its environs witnessed many gold seekers, explorers, covered wagons, and stage coaches on their way West. This expanding desert community has plenty of shops, restaurants, motels, and a nearby airport, and is adjacent to China Lake Naval Weapons Center.

It is situated on State 178 just off US 395 about 150mi (240km) north east of Los Angeles.

Riverside L13

Best known for its 550-acre raceway which attracts world famous racing drivers to compete in five major races a year. They are: the Winston Western 500, Camel GT Six Hours of Riverside, Tuborg 400, AC-Delco World Championship of Off-Road Racing and Riverside Grand Prix and International Race of Champions.

See also Mission Inn on 7th St, a 102-year-old state and national monument containing $1\frac{1}{2}$ million worth of antiques, nine orginal Tiffany windows, and a 17th-century hand-carved gold-leaf altar. Rooms are available here year round.

San Bernardino K13

Site of an annual agricultural fair each spring to commemorate the citrus crop harvest in Southern California. During the 11-day event, there are citrus exhibits and museum, a rodeo, flower show, free stage shows, cooking contests, continuous entertainment, pageants, and parades.

San Bernardino has a Holiday Inn among other accommodations and is close to the mountains as well as Big Bear Lake and Lake Arrowhead, both recreational areas.

San Diego Q13

History 'The Birthplace' of California was discovered in 1542 by Juan Rodriguez Cabrillo, a Portuguese explorer in the service of Spain who sailed into San Diego Bay and named it San Miguel. (It wasn't given its present name until 60 years later, by Vizcaino.) And it wasn't until 1769 that

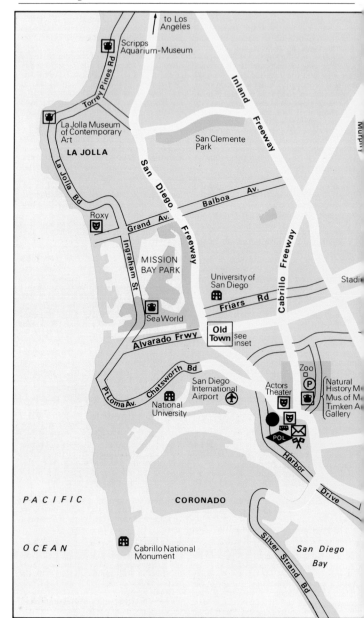

to Los Angeles

Scripps Aquarium-Museum

Torrey Pines Rd

Inland Freeway

La Jolla Museum of Contemporary Art

LA JOLLA

San Clemente Park

San Diego Freeway

Balboa Av.

La Jolla Bd

Roxy

Grand Av.

Ingraham St

Cabrillo Freeway

MISSION BAY PARK

University of San Diego

Friars Rd

Stadi

Murphy

SeaWorld

Alvarado Frwy

Old Town see inset

Chatsworth Bd

Pt Loma Av.

San Diego International Airport

Actors Theater

Zoo

P

Natural History M
Mus. of M
Timken A
Gallery

National University

POL

PACIFIC

CORONADO

Harbor

Drive

OCEAN

Cabrillo National Monument

Silver Strand Bd

San Diego Bay

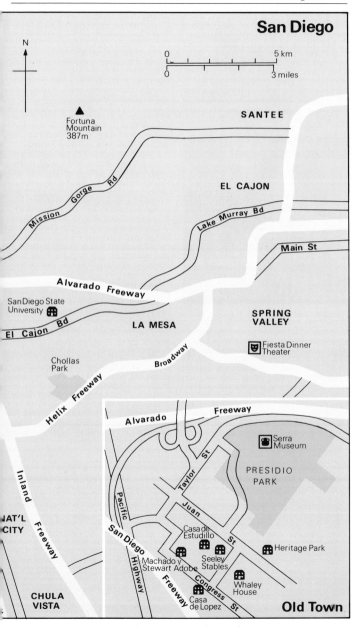

San Diego

N

0 ____ 5 km
0 ____ 3 miles

▲ Fortuna Mountain 387m

SANTEE

EL CAJON

Mission Gorge Rd

Lake Murray Bd

Main St

Alvarado Freeway

San Diego State University

El Cajon Bd

LA MESA

SPRING VALLEY

Fiesta Dinner Theater

Chollas Park

Broadway

Helix Freeway

Alvarado Freeway

Serra Museum

PRESIDIO PARK

Taylor St

Juan St

Pacific

Casa de Estudillo

Heritage Park

San Diego Highway

Machado y Stewart Adobe

Seeley Stables

Freeway

Congress St

Whaley House

Casa de Lopez

Old Town

Inland Freeway

NAT'L CITY

CHULA VISTA

the first in the chain of missions, and a settlement was established under Father Junipero Serra and Gaspar de Portola.

In 1810, the Mexicans gained control of San Diego but trade didn't pick up in the area until after 1821 and in 1825, San Diego was the Mexican capital of California, with a town developed round the central plaza. In 1846, the Americans took over when they defeated the Mexicans at the Battle of San Pascual and raised the US flag for the first time in California, in San Diego's plaza.

Junipero Serra Museum, San Diego

San Diego grew only slowly, taking a back seat to Los Angeles and San Francisco. It more or less remained an insular village until the move was made from the 'Old Town' to the new town at harbor-side. Its dwindling population lost it its first 1850 charter which was not regained until some years later. But once the railroad came to San Diego in 1885, it flourishing enough for the US Navy to make it their base in 1897.

The Panama-California Exposition in 1915 to celebrate the opening of the Panama Canal, and the 1935 California-Pacific International Exposition, were both responsible for the development of one of San Diego's highlights – Balboa Park. The present size of the naval complex here is due to World War II, when naval headquarters were moved here from Honolulu. After the war, many of those who had passed through, returned to settle. Aircraft companies moved into the space age – aerospace equipment and missiles are today's number two industry. (San Diego gave birth to the Atlas missile, one of the earliest sophisticated rockets.) Agriculture is the fourth largest industry in the county, with the production of millions of avocadoes among other things.

Accommodations There are resort hotels, convention hotels and many lower-priced motels in various districts of San Diego. TraveLodge Tower and Sheraton Harbor Island Hotel are tops on Harbor Island, a man-made recreational area that is much closer to the airport and downtown than it seems. The island is a resort in itself with shops, malls, restaurants, and beachside proms.

Half Moon Inn is one of the best on another man-made island in the bay, Shelter Island, which is lined with marinas and boat yards. Others in the vicinity include: Kona Inn and Marina Inn.

Downtown is not without deluxe properties. Little America Westgate is decorated with $1 million of antiques and its Fontainebleau Room is one of downtown's finest restaurants. Town and Country is large, but one of the best properties in Mission Valley, another area flanked by hotels, shops, and places to eat.

Landmark hotel is the Del Coronado on an authentic island in the bay (but joined via a causeway). It has hosted presidents and celebrities and is such a rambling building that non-resident guests may take a tour of it.

Since San Diego is TraveLodge headquarters, there are TraveLodge hotels and motels all over the town and county, including the Mission Bay beaches. Other chain names present include: Holiday Inn, Ramada and Rodeway for comfortable moderate lodgings.

Eating Out San Diego is most noted for its choice of seafood and Mexican restaurants – Mexico is just down the road and across the border, after all. Two local chain establishments to look out for are Anthony's Fish Grottos and Chart House.

One of the West Coast's best seafood restaurants is Anthony's Star of the Sea Room overlooking the harbour. Clams Genovese is only one of their specialities and the fresh abalone is delicious. Lubach's is another first class place for fish and duck dishes, although it has too much competition to hold *the* top title as it once did. Try the Aztec Dining Rooms for Mexican combination plates.

Entertainment 'Class' nightlife is really only to be found in the hotels and the better restaurants where guitarists or violinists serenade. A number of hotel lounges feature Polynesian-style shows such as the Bali Hai South Pacific Room and the Polynesian Room at the Catamaran. Top hotels have music for dancing and there are some 'intimé' bars in nearby La Jolla.

Most of the downtown clubs are of the topless, go-go and strip variety along Lower Broadway.

Old Town, San Diego

Sport Watersports predominate since San Diego can justifiably boast of thousands of acres of protected waters in its two bays. The mild year-round climate allows them to be enjoyed at any season. There are public boat launch facilities at Mission Bay, San Diego Bay, and Oceanside Small Craft Harbor. Almost any type of boat may be rented at the marinas or from hotels like the Bahia, Catamaran, Del Coronado, Islandia Hyatt House, or Vacation Village.

Certain parts of Mission Bay have been specifically designated for skiers. The east end of the South Pacific Passage can be used for jet skis and waterskis can be used in the east bay area. A variety of beach equipment, including surfboards, may be rented from Ocean Beach, Mission Beach, Pacific Beach, and La Jolla.

Year-round ocean fishing is a key feature. Party and special charter boats leave from both bays and many rendezvous at the Mexican-owned Coronado Islands, 18mi (28km) out to sea. A fishing license is needed for fishing Californian waters, available from the California Dept. of Fish and Game, 1350 Front St, San Diego, CA 92101 (714 237 7311). San Diego has one of the most modern sport-fishing fleets in the world.

With a license, anyone can fish the 70mi (113km) shoreline (except for swimming areas), but no license is required for pier fishing.

San Diego equally has a good name for tennis and golfing facilities, both public and private. Other sports available include horse racing at nearby Del Mar, baseball, basketball, football, and soccer. Hunting grunion is another activity from June 1 to March 31 (with a license). Grunion are, in fact, tiny silversided fish which are caught by hand when they make their run. They can be hunted along the shoreline in Imperial Beach, Silver Strand, Ocean Beach, La Jolla, Torrey Pines, and the unlit areas of Pacific Beach.

Old Town In 1969, California's birthplace – six and a half blocks of Old Town – were set aside as a historic state park, to restore and preserve San Diego's heritage. A walking tour is the best way to see the 12-acre park, either by yourself or on an organized trip. The state park itself and the Old Town Historical Society both offer free tours. Those led by park rangers depart daily at 1400 from the Machada y Silvas Adobe across from the plaza. The others, covering 25 historical sites, leave at 1300 on Sat. from the Whaley House, 2482 San Diego Ave.

Restored buildings include the **Casa de Estudillo** which was made from logs brought from the mountains and rawhide for securing beams (1830), and the **Machado/Stewart Adobe**. A number of the renovated buildings now house interesting 'collections' such as **Casa De Lopez** which is an attractive candle shop and the **Casa de Altamirano**, a New England-style frame house which has become a newspaper museum. Horse-drawn vehicles and western memorabilia are on show at the **Seeley Stables**, a former stage line terminal. The **Whaley House** was the first luxury two-storey brick home to be built in San Diego (1856) and has been lovingly restored with antiques and period furnishings. **Presidio Park**, site of the first mission overlooks the Old Town (see Missions).

Other attractions First stop should be at the **Cabrillo National Monument** which commemorates Cabrillo's discovery of the Californian coast in 1542, but also gives a magnificent view of San Diego Bay. The Visitor's Center shows Cabrillo's explorations and discoveries.

The most historic structure here is the **Lighthouse** which was first lit in 1855, and served for 40 years as an aid to passing ships. In 1891, a new one was built at the water's edge and is still operated. Behind the original lighthouse is an observation point for watching the annual migration of whales. From December to February, thousands of California greys make their way south, heading for Baja's warm lagoons. Whales can be spotted from a glassed-in observatory containing whale exhibits and supplying a taped description of their habits. The Monument at the tip of Point Loma is open daily from 0900–1715, and to 1945 in summer.

Lighthouse, Cabrillo National Monument

A different kind of observatory is **Palomar** on top of Mt Palomar. It's America's largest telescope, with a range of one billion light years. It utilizes mirrors, not a lens, and is in effect a huge camera. The telescope may be viewed from the visitor's gallery in the observatory and photographs taken from it are displayed in the nearby exhibit hall. Open daily 0900–1700.

Palomar Observatory

Not only is San Diego Bay home port for America's navy and a sportfishing base – it is also beautiful enough to make a cruise of it a pleasure. Harbor activities may be inspected via a San Diego Harbor cruise excursion, by Coast Marine Services, or on the barquentine *California* – perhaps the most fun. It departs from Sheraton Harbor Island Hotel dock, offers a main season from March through mid December although it also features whale-watching cruises during winter.

Shopping – if only the window kind – is appealing in the Old Town at **Squibob Square** and **Bazaar del Mundo** where boutiques and craft shops can be found. On the outskirts of Old Town, **Heritage Park** features more of the same in a Victorian style. Unusual gifts can be found in the Burton House, a family home built in 1893, in the Sherman-Gilbert House, and in the Bushyhead House (1887). The Queen Anne-style Christian House (1889) is a restaurant while public restrooms are to be found in Senlis Cottage. The **Gaslamp Quarter**, downtown, also reflects the Victorian era with its restored buildings and shops now filled with antiques, arts, and crafts. Down at the waterfront, **Marina Village** and **Seaport Village** sell a range of goods from nautical accessories to handcrafted items. Local artists and craftsmen's work may also be found (along with the fresh produce) at **Farmers Bazaar** on Seventh Ave, located in the old Western Metal Warehouse.

And lest we forget Mexico, **Tijuana** is a popular excursion for visitors to San Diego, whether for entertainment, tacos, or shopping. Tijuana is a free port and while it is not Mexico's most beautiful town, it has lots of color and excitement.

San Diego's two parks are ideal for a day out. **Balboa Park** is located in the heart of the city and covers more than ,000 acres. Within it are museums, art galleries, theaters, sports facilities and the zoo (see Young West Coast). The park's museum complex is an exceptionally good one. All the buildings are within walking distance of one another. The complex includes the Reuben Fleet Space Theater (see Young West Coast), Hall of Champions, Museum of Man, Natural History Museum, San Diego Museum of Art and the Timken Art Gallery (see Museums). (Only Washington D.C. has a similar centralized complex.)

Many of the Spanish-Moorish buildings are left over from the Panama-California Exposition of 1915 and the California-Pacific International Exposition of 1935. One of the best examples of this type of architecture is the California Tower whose 100-bell carillon chimes each quarter of an hour, and is a city landmark.

Mission Bay Park, several miles north of the Bay, was nothing more than marshland when Cabrillo entered these parts. Who could have known then that it would eventually be transformed into a 4,600 acre aquatic park and playground. It is one of the largest facilities of its kind in the world, devoted to water sports and amusements.

Boating is the most popular activity – rental available from the marinas. Halibut, bass, and flounder are among the fish one can expect to catch from its waters and sportfishing boats leave from here for the Pacific waters on half or full-day expeditions. **Sea World** (see Young West Coast) is at home here.

For swimmers and sunbathers, there are 26mi (43km) of beaches with nine off-limit-to-boats swim areas. Behind the sand are grassy picnic areas.

California Tower, Balboa Park

San Marcos   P13

San Marcos is an agricultural center with numerous orchards and poultry ranches. Midway between Vista and Escondido, its main attraction is lake San Marcos.

It is 40mi (64km) north of San Diego on State 78 off Interstate 15 at Escondido.

San Juan Capistrano   N12

The place the swallows return to – the mission here is famous (see Missions). The city has grown around the mission to become a popular resort 30 minutes from Disneyland, taking its name from St. John Capistran. There are several places to stay like the Best Western Capistrano Inn.

You can reach San Juan Capistrano, 56mi (90km) south of Los Angeles, by Interstate 5, the Santa Ana Freeway, or Interstate 405, the San Diego Freeway, or along the coast on State 1, the Pacific Coast Highway.

Santa Ana   M11

The county seat of Orange County and its second largest city, Santa Ana is located on the Santa Ana Freeway. Motels include the Vagabond, the Ramada, and a TraveLodge. Interesting nightlife includes the Harlequin Dinner Playhouse, more elegant than many with a choice of buffet or served six-course meal plus stage show. Also the Kono Hawaii's dinner shows with a Hawaiian theme.

In the vicinity is the **Bowers Museum** which contains items relevant to Southern California's history. Additionally, there are Mexican, Aztec, and Mayan antiquities among the 2,500,000 art and history objects. To reach it, take the Main St exit from the Santa Ana Freeway; turn right and travel on about a half mile to 20th St and Main. Open Tues.–Sat. 0900–1700; Sun, 1200–1700.

Dana Point Harbor can be visited as well – easy to reach from anywhere in Orange County (opposite for directions to San Juan Capistrano). It's a recreational port with two marinas in a natural cove beneath the cliffs. The place takes its name

Santa Barbara Mission

from Richard Henry Dana who called it 'the only romantic spot on the coast'. It's a home port for some 2,500 yachts and for the visitor there are motels, restaurants, and speciality shopping villages lining the waterways. From here you can go sportfishing, whale watching, swimming – or just relax. In the old clipper days, this used to be the only trading post between San Diego and Santa Barbara.

Santa Barbara J5

A resort city with a heavy Spanish influence to be seen in its handsome adobes and its missions (see Missions). Buildings still have red tiled roofs and Moorish doorways as they did 200 odd years ago.

There's a yacht harbor, good ocean swimming, and amusements for all the family in Santa Barbara. Family-priced motels include several Best Westerns, Vagabond, and a TraveLodge. A good choice of restaurants and sports make this a popular centre often referred to as 'America's Riviera', for it has a beautiful setting between the Pacific Coast and the Santa Ynez mountains.

While here, see the Santa Barbara Botanic Garden on Mission Canyon Rd. It covers 65 acres and is devoted entirely to Californian shrubs, trees, and flowers. Five miles (8km) of trail wind through the garden and a guided tour is given on Thurs. at 1030. Open 0800 to sunset.

The Santa Barbara Zoological Gardens combines park, children's playground, and zoo. Located one block south of Highway 101 on E. Cabrillo Bvd, this was once the site of a Chumash Indian village. It became a private estate in the 1900s and was donated to the city. Open year round Tues.–Sun. 1000–1630.

One of the city's most historic buildings is the County Courthouse which occupies a city block. Inside, there are decorated ceilings, historic exhibits, wrought iron chandeliers, carved doors, and Tunisian tiling. An excellent city view is obtained from its 70ft (21m) clock tower. Open weekdays 0800–1700.

Restaurant, Santa Barbara

Santa Monica   L9

A famous Greater Los Angeles beach resort with three miles (4.8km) of good sandy beaches. It was already a resort in the 1870s because of its ideal year-round climate, and today it is a residential and convention city besides. It may be reached from the city via any of four major boulevards: Wilshire, Santa Monica, Olympic, and Pico, all of which lead to the ocean and the 14-block long Palisades Park.

It is a 'fun' place with plenty of amusements, hotels and motels along the coast. Fishing, boating, and swimming are available at the Santa Monica Pier. Like Malibu, it attracted the stars of the thirties and some of their palatial homes are still to be seen along the beach. Santa Monica is bounded by San Vicente Blvd to the north and by Venice to the south.

Accommodations include a Holiday Inn adjacent to the pier and the Surf Rider Inn on Ocean Ave. The Old Venice Noodle Co. is one of those restaurants where the decor is eclectic to say the least (on Main St) whilst Chez Jay on Ocean Ave offers typical California food.

Solvang   J3

A city whose name means 'sunny field', founded by Danish settlers in 1911. The atmosphere is rural but strongly Scandinavian with cobblestoned walks and windmills. Buildings are constructed Danish-style with bindingsvaerk walls, simulated thatch or copper roofs, and stained-glass windows. Many of the restaurants and bakeries feature Danish cuisine and pastries and each September (the third weekend) a festival is held here when all the residents wear Danish national dress. On the outskirts of Solvang is another visitor's must – the mission of Santa Ines built in 1804 (see Missions).

Solvang is about 140mi (225km) west of Los Angeles just off US 101 on State 154. Santa Ines is 4mi (6.5km) east on 154.

Topanga   L9

A naturalist's retreat midway between Malibu and Santa Monica – the Topanga Canyon, interesting for a side excursion or a quiet weekend at an inn. Discovery Inn is a rustic place that serves exceptionally fine food, on South Topanga Canyon Blvd, while the Inn of the Seventh Ray on Old Topanga Canyon Rd is a 'natural food' restaurant.

Vista   O13

The city takes its name from the Spanish for 'view' and many of its hillside homes have just that – a beautiful view. It lies in an area of avocado and citrus groves and has a small town friendliness and charm.

Situated 36mi (54km) north of San Diego, Vista is 6mi (10km) east of Carlsbad on State 78.

Ventura   K6

Formerly just a tiny mission, today a busy city surrounded by citrus and avocado groves. Along with the San Buenaventura Mission, see the Ventura County Historical Museum on Main St, which shows pioneer Spanish and Indian relics, and the Olivas Adobe, a restored hacienda on Olivas Park Dr.

San Buenaventura State Beach takes up 116 acres of sheltered coast and is good for watersports and fishing. Sporting activity is also available at the Emma Ward State Beach and the McGrath State Beach, with boating from Ventura harbor. Plentiful accommodation includes Holiday Inn, Vagabond Motel, and TraveLodge. Ventura has its own County Fair each October.

Ventura is about 70mi (113km) west of Los Angeles on US 101.

Santa Monica Beach

SAN FRANCISCO

History The bay of San Francisco was sighted and noted on several occasions during the early exploratory expeditions into California, but it wasn't until the Mission of San Francisco de Asis was founded in 1776 that any real settlement began. At the time, the cove was known as 'Yerba Buena' and it wasn't until 1845 that it became known officially by today's name.

A number of missions were established in the vicinity in the 18th century and ranches gradually grew up between them. The first urban development was due to trade potential and merchants swelled the hamlet's population. In four years – between 1845 and 1849, the population grew from 150 to 1000. In the early 19th century there were New England whalers and Russian trappers in what can only be called a shanty town – with mud streets and rickety shacks.

In 1849, gold was discovered at Sutter's Fort and San Francisco was never quite the same. Everyone wanted to strike it rich. The wagons rolled and adventurers from around the world headed for the Golden West. Mines and the new railroad brought in masses of immigrants, especially the Chinese. Little Chinatown may have only been an embryo on Upper Sacramento Street and Dupont Street in 1850, but it rapidly expanded. Opium dens and brothels flourished and no amount of government bills managed to restrict the growth of the Chinese population.

The finding of silver in the Comstock Lode also brought prosperity and immigrants, ten years later. Between 1850 and 1870, San Francisco gained a cosmopolitan atmosphere – one it has never lost. It became the terminus for the Pony Express in 1860 and of the Trans-Continental Railroad in 1869.

In the wake of the Gold Rush came violence and crime and that resulted in the formation of the Vigilantes. The 1856 Committee had 6,000 members. While there was quick profit to be made in the saloons and gambling parlors, after the Gold Rush, many miners turned to banking, farming, or fishing, giving the city its first opportunity as a banking center.

Precious metal and the fortunes made from it were the key to San Francisco's development. The transportation system improved and grand mansions were built. the arts flourished – by 1870 culture was an 'in' word and from 1879 the city's Tivoli Theater and Opera House featured opera year-round. By the end of the 19th century, the Opera Season was America's finest. Music was so popular that San Francisco's symphony orchestra was the first in America to receive regular aid from public funds. San Francisco also boasted California's first municipal school system.

In the late 19th century, the city had earned itself a good name for fine food and accommodation and many a gold-plate banquet was held in the Palace Hotel, the same place where Diamond Jim Brady consumed six dozen oysters at one fell swoop.

Since its early days when the majority of the structures were made of wood, San Francisco has been subject to and suffered from fires, but the one in 1906, caused by the infamous earthquake, was a real blockbuster. The three-day fire left Nob Hill and Chinatown in ruins and destroyed most of the city's business houses, banks, churches, and newspapers. Property loss that year was estimated to be $200,000,000.

Despite the setback, such damage gave incentive for a new and better city rebuilding program and also helped the growth of the adjacent communities. Transport systems once again benefited with the arrival of the car – improved highways and a whole avenue (Van Ness) devoted to car dealers – and after 1915, the Key Route Electric Railway to serve the East Bay area and supplement the Peninsular Electric Railway. During the twenties and thirties, San Francisco became a true metropolis. The Bay bridges were built and Golden Gate Park, improved. The shipyards, dry docks, canneries, and other industries expanded.

The city survived the nation-wide depression years and the Second World War. It even survived the hippy disturbances of the sixties in its Haight-Ashbury district. But it is still a melting pot for numerous nationalities as it was in its

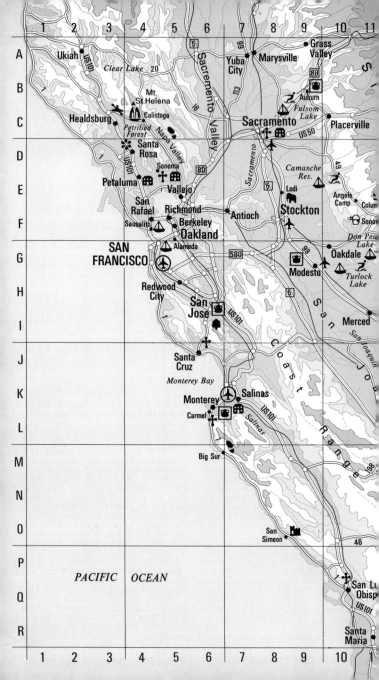

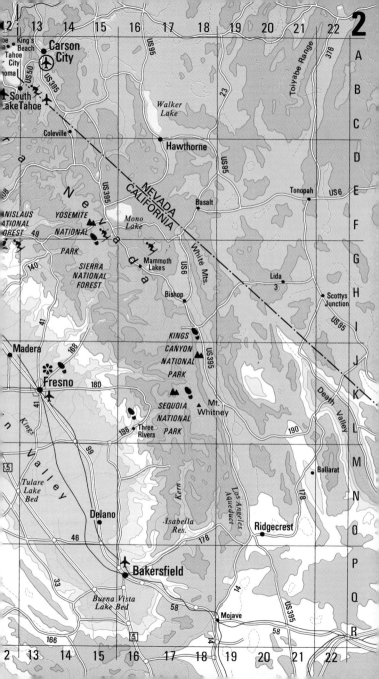

Gold Rush days. It still likes bawdy entertainment (as the miners did) and it still has that special tolerance to all aspects of life, one of the reasons it has a large gay community. Even the two-year drought in the seventies was borne with good humour, and the thought that the San Andreas Fault could again move doesn't cause concern. Nor does it stop Americans saying this is their favorite city.

Accommodations Among the ritziest are those hotels on Nob Hill. The Mark Hopkins at No. 1 Nob Hill retains some of the gables and turrets of railroad magnate Mark Hopkins' original home. It is expensive, elegant and perhaps best known for its Top of the Mark lounge, which has a 360° panoramic view of the city. Opposite is another gracious hotel, the Fairmont, first built for another successful man, James Fair. Also pricey and fashionable, the distinctive old main building has a modern tower adjoining it. A good choice of restaurants and bars including the Fairmont Crown and Venetian Room supper club. Stanford Court on California St, also in Nob Hill tradition, was built on the site of Leland Stanford's opulent mansion. This top bracket hotel features such 'extras' as mini TVs in the bathrooms, free local telephone calls and gift boxes of Godiva chocolates.

Also luxurious are: Hyatt Regency at Embarcadero Center (there's another Hyatt on Union Square) with an atrium lobby and a top revolving bar with a great view. The Clift on Geary and Taylor Sts is more subdued but elite while the St Francis is *the* Union Square landmark. It has been hosting celebrities since 1904 and still keeps its rosewood and crystal image.

Among the more moderate accommodations are the Canterbury on Sutter St which houses in its favor, Lehr's Greenhouse restaurant, a popular San Francisco rendezvous. The Washington Square Inn on Stockton St is tiny but charming. In the reasonably priced Drake Wiltshire also on Stockton St, guests can have a shiatsu massage. And there is old fashioned service at the low priced Hotel Beresford on Sutter St.

Eating Out There are literally hundreds of good restaurants in San Francisco. The city's home base of Trader Vic's (which has since branched out all over the country). Many of them specialize in seafood, from the take away food stalls at the waterfront to sit down silver service. Among the best of the latter are: Ernie's on Montgomery St, a long established restaurant of note, which has introduced *nouvelle cuisine* into its Victorian setting. Or there's Le Club, an expensive place

tucked away in a Nob Hill apartment block where the food's French and anything can be prepared in addition to the classic menu. A landmark cafe that doesn't cost a lot is the Buena Vista, said to make the best Irish coffee in town since the drinking takes precedence over the eating here! A moderately priced dining spot that is also a landmark is Jack's on Sacramento St. The decor's not special, but the grills are good and the banana fritters with brandy sauce, superb. David's on Geary St is excellent for anyone who enjoys lashing of chicken liver and cheese blintzes with sour cream; Jewish cuisine that's delicious and not costly. That original Trader Vic's, on Cosmo Pl. will need the credit cards but the international menu is extensive and the Polynesian decor and drinks worth it. Doro's, Montgomery St, features Italian and French food in excellent fashion. Takeaway shops, coffee shops and chain food shops like Macdonald's are plentiful.

Geary Street, San Francisco

Entertainment Most of the top live entertainment is to be found in hotel nightclubs like the Fairmont's Venetian Room. Hotels are the best places for dancing, too, whether the romantic kind – try the Starlite Roof of the Sir Francis Drake – or disco, say at Nappertandy's at the Union Square Hyatt. San Francisco likes jazz and there's a good choice of places where one can listen to it. Earthquake McGoon's at the Embarcadero is currently good while well-known jazz artists are likely to appear at Great American Music Hall on O'Farrell.

San Francisco also offers sleazier nightlife, especially along Broadway where flashing neon signs promote topless bars, strip shows, encounter parlors etc. North Beach area 'glitters' with it all. One Broadway landmark that is worth going to is Finocchio's whose female impersonators are first class.

The Arts San Francisco has always attracted artists and writers. Some visited, like Oscar Wilde. Some visited and stayed a while, like Mark Twain who lived in the city for a spell as a reporter on the *San Francisco Morning Call*. Anthony Trollope, Rudyard Kipling, and William Saroyan were all impressed by the place in different ways.

Theater and music have flourished since the Gold Rush Days. Today, the Golden Gate Theater at Golden Gate and Taylor Sts puts on Broadway productions and the Curran Theater often stages travelling Broadway shows. Musical revues can be seen at the On-Broadway Theater.

The San Francisco Opera Company performs at the War Memorial Opera House as does the Symphony Orchestra. The latter sometimes gives free Sunday concerts in summer at Stern Grove. The San Francisco Ballet Troupe can equally be seen performing at the Opera House.

Sport Baseball can be watched in Candlestick Park where the Giants play home games from April to October. Football is played here from August to December. Bay Meadows, in San Mateo, is the place for racing. Golf courses and tennis courts are to be found in Golden Gate Park which also has seven miles (11km) of riding trails. Roller skates, too, may be rented in the park. Salmon fishing is possible in the Bay in season, from mid February to mid October.

Walking Tours

Downtown start off at one of the busiest streets – **Powell St** where the Powell Cable Car Turntable is. Walk north and you'll quickly come to the downtown focal point, **Union Square**, the heart of the

Union Square, San Francisco

shopping district. It's an ideal meeting place or resting place (there are benches) and each July 4 a cable car bell ringing contest takes place. The 2.6 acre block was presented to the city by John Geary (who has a street named for him, also bordering the square), San Francisco's last mayor under the Spanish system.

If you cross Stockton St at Post St, you'll come to **Maiden Lane** which used to be the Red Light District back in the 1800s. Nowadays, this two-block-long street is a pleasant one lined with little restaurants and shops. Originally it was Morton St. Its name changed to Union Square Avenue in 1909 and in 1922 it was renamed Maiden Lane after New York's silver and jewellery trade center.

Walk a half block south on Kearny St (named for General Stephen Watts Kearny) to the junction of Market, Geary and Kearny Sts, and you'll see **Lotta's Fountain**. The Lotta in question was Lotta Crabtree who was taught to sing and dance by the notorious Lola Montez.

Go up Market St and you'll reach **Montgomery St**, San Francisco's financial centre. On the way up the latter, you'll cross another major street – Sutter, named for the Swiss adventurer, Johann Sutter. At the intersection is the Sutter Building on the site of one of the city's most famous early hotels, Lick House.

A number of skyscrapers flank Montgomery. The **Mills Building**, for example was built by one of the founders of the Bank of California. The **Russ Building**, across the street was at one time the city's tallest. The **Pacific Coast Stock Exchange**, at the corner of Pine and Sansome streets, is one of the more impressive buildings. Its visitor's gallery is open from 0700–1430 on weekdays. Another monument to finance is the headquarters of **Bank of America**, a block large institution.

Wells Fargo Bank's History Room is well worth a look in, open 1000–1500 on regular banking days. Here are mementoes of some of San Francisco's more colorful characters like highwayman, Black Bart, and the Vigilantes. The collection covers the period from 1852, when the company was formed, to 1906.

The plaque at the corner of Montgomery and Clay Sts commemorates the site of the founding of the Society of California Pioneers, organized in 1850 to collect the state's history. (The Society's present location is on McAllister St.) The two plaques on the corner of Montgomery and Merchant Sts relate to the Pony Express: one to mark the arrival of the first rider, and the other to mark the headquarters of the Pony Express agents.

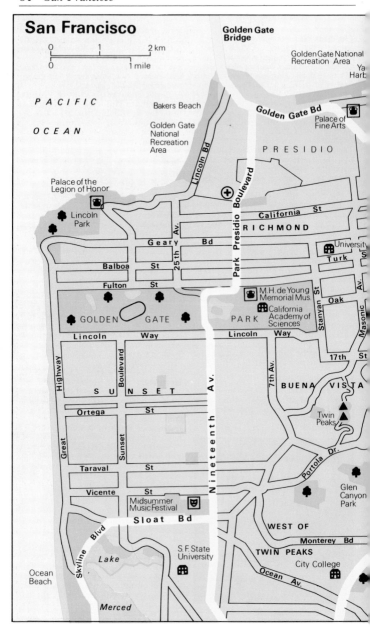

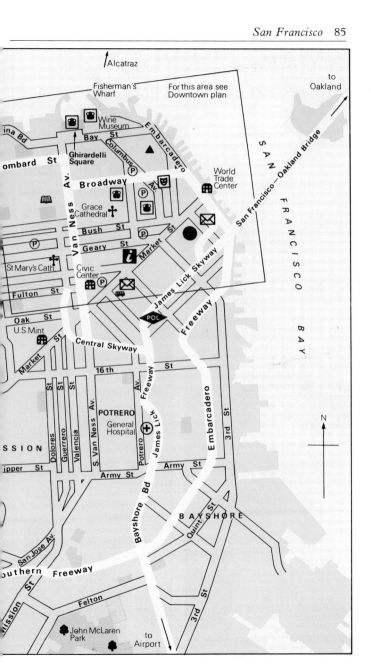

Victorian houses, San Francisco

Coit Tower, San Francisco

Hearst Castle, San Simeon

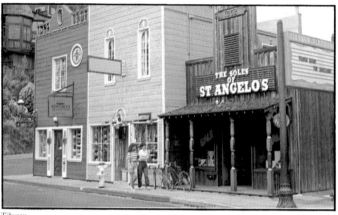

Tiburon

Victorian building and Transamerica Building

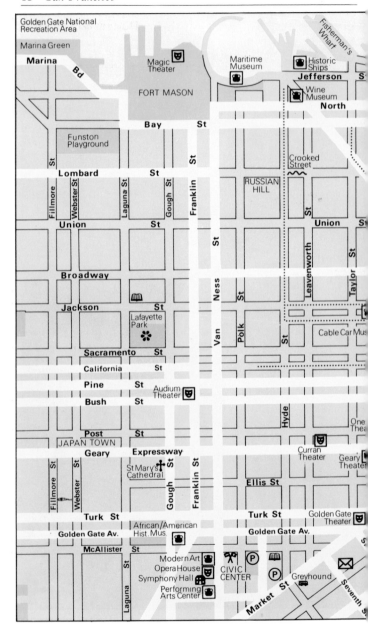

Downtown Fr'isco

Pier 39

0   1/2   1 km

0   1/2 mile

·········· Cable Car routes

N

The Embarcadero

int St

ay St

Lombard St

▲ Telegraph Hill

The Embarcadero

Club Fugazi
NORTH BEACH
Ⓟ
Phoenix Theater
roadway
On Broadway

Sansome St

Battery St

Montgomery St

Jackson

Stockton St

Ⓟ Washington St Ⓟ

Clay St

FINANCIAL

Sacramento St

California St

Wax Museum

Mus. of Money

DISTRICT

CHINA
TOWN
ine St
ush St

Kearny St

Embarcadero Freeway

Steuart St

Main St

Beale St

First St

✉

Ⓟ Post St

Powell St

Market St

Second St

Transbay Transit Terminal ●

Ⓟ Geary St

Ⓟ

Third St

Fourth St

Mission St

Howard St

Downtown Art Center

San Francisco–Oakland Bridge

Old U.S. Mint

Fifth St

Folsom St

St

Bryant St

Brannan St

Bank of Canton, Chinatown, San Francisco

Montgomery St is a long one with a fascinating history. At the top of it, walk one block west on Washington St to **Portsmouth Square**. In the 1800s, there were public hangings here, gambling houses, the city's first hotel and the Jenny Lind Theater. Today, it is just another quiet city square.

Chinatown is downtown with **Grant Avenue** its major artery. Walk north from Market St and you'll pass a host of colorful Chinese shops once you've 'entered' the Chinese stronghold at Bush St where an ornamental green-tiled gate stands. Go east on Pine St and you'll come to the **Kong Chow Temple**, one of the few surviving joss houses; 'joss' being a corruption of the word 'dios'. This temple is dedicated to the military god, Kwan Ti, and contains many beautiful wood carvings, brocades, and items of worship.

Pine St borders **St Mary's Square**.

The statue here is of Dr Sun Yat-sen, founder of the Chinese Republic, and is made of granite and stainless steel, sculpted by Beniamino Bufano. The square itself is a peaceful oasis amid the bustle of Chinatown although it used to be the location of the worst brothels and gambling saloons.

Old St Mary's Church on Grant Ave at California St was built with granite brought from China, and has a four-faced clock tower. After the 1906 fire, its interior was restored. When you get to Grant Ave and Washington St, turn east. That three-tiered building that looks like a pagoda, is in fact the **Bank of Canton**, but at one time housed the Chinese Telephone Exchange. **Buddha's Universal Church**, at the corner of Washington and Kearny Sts, contains a large research library devoted to Chinese philosophy and religion.

View from Telegraph Hill, San Francisco

Just west of Grant Ave. is **Waverly Place**, a narrow alley which used to be as notorious as St Mary's Square for its brothels and gambling dens. It was often the site of Tong battles, but today it is one of Chinatown's prettiest streets. the **Tin How Temple** is a joss house dedicated to a goddess who protects travellers.

Chinatown is full of interesting little back alleys, shops selling all kinds of Orientalia, tea houses, and some very fine restaurants. During Chinese holidays, Chinatown is at its brightest, particularly on Chinese National Day when there is a dragon parade along Grant Ave, and at Chinese New Year when similarly there are lion dances and dragon parades.

Telegraph Hill-North Beach Start at the northern end of Montgomery St where the **California Steam and Navigation Building** stands. It dates from 1859 and survived the Big Fire as did the

Ship Building (which houses Doro's Restaurant) and several other old buildings in the vicinity. Walk east on Jackson St and you'll pass the interior decorators' center, art galleries and shops. Go west on Jackson and you'll come to Columbus Ave. (The area bounded by Montgomery, Pacific, Washington and Kearny Sts, and intersected by Columbus Ave, is **Little Manila**.) **Columbus Tower** at Kearny and Columbus is one of several flatiron buildings on the avenue.

Going east on Pacific Ave you'll be in what was known as the Barbary Coast – full of dance halls and dives of one kind or another. The 1906 fire destroyed practically all the Barbary Coast, but it was still the first to be back in business afterwards, if on a smaller scale. The B girls and bars lasted until the 50s, but these days it's more an annexe to the interior decorators of Jackson St.

Continue up Columbus Ave, and you'll be in North Beach, so called because back in the 1860s, there was a beach here before San Francisco started filling in land along this part of the bay. This is **Little Italy**. It also contains the jazziest nightlife belt – **Broadway**. The restaurants, bars, and clubs run the gamut from low grade to good quality and come in every ethnic guise.

Cross Broadway and head north along Grant Ave to Union St. Follow the latter west to **Washington Square**. One of the statues here is of Benjamin Franklin and was donated to the city by a millionaire pioneer dentist. The Volunteer Firemen's Monument, in bronze, comprising a group of three fireman making a rescue, was donated by Lillie Hitchcock Coit, daughter of a prominent surgeon.

It was her money which paid for **Coit Tower** on top of nearby Telegraph Hill. The hill is 274ft (83m) above sea level and the tower rises 210ft (64m) from its summit. Take the lift to the top for one of the best views in the city. Or stay in Pioneer Park, at its base. On a clear day, you can see beyond the Golden Gate Bridge to Sausalito, the Bay and its islands, Berkeley, and the East Bay Hills – with downtown San Francisco and Nob and Russian Hills to the west.

Washington Square, San Francisco

Telegraph Hill and Coit Tower, San Francisco

Mason Street, San Francisco

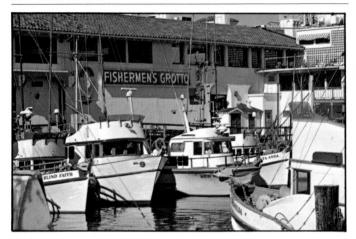

Fisherman's Wharf, San Francisco

The Waterfront – start at the foot of Taylor St, the location of **Fisherman's Wharf**, a tourist mecca. It's an area to love or hate ... gaudy and garish and none of the authenticity that the wharves here used to have. There are fish markets where you can purchase steaming shrimp and crab, good fish restaurants, souvenir shops and pavement stalls, hawking anything from badges to hand-made jewellery. Street entertainers (out for the tourist dollar) are almost out in force along the waterfront.

Two turnabout cable car points are at the Victorian Plaza and Fisherman's Wharf, near to the **Maritime Museum** at the foot of Beach and Polk Sts. One block east at **Hyde St Pier**, several early Californian boats are moored. Visit also **Ghirardelli Square**. This old chocolate factory was cleverly converted into a multi-level complex of boutiques and restaurants. Similarly, **The Cannery** is a half-block shopping complex, converted from an old fruit canning plant.

Pier 39 is a complex on the **Embarcadero**, not to be missed. What is called the Embarcadero is the area from Fisherman's Wharf to the Ferry Building. Boats depart on sightseeing excursions from the piers here. For Bay cruises, use Pier 43½. Helicopters operate from Pier 43, along which is berthed the **Balclutha**, a square rigger which made her maiden voyage in 1887 around the Horn, and is now an historical exhibit for viewing.

Boats also leave for a tour of **Alcatraz**, the Bay's infamous island. Although no longer used as a prison, it gained its reputation as 'The Rock' because it was

considered impenetrable. It actually housed its first prisoners in the Civil War and among the 'names' it has held were Al Capone and Machine Gun Kelly.

The largest island in the Bay is **Angel Island**, now a state park. It was the landing spot of the first ship to sail through the Golden Gate and was given the name Nuestra Senora de los Angeles before Los Angeles took it. Only a small portion of **Yerba Buena Island** is open to the public as the majority of it is a naval base. **Treasure Island** is connected but was man-made for the 1939 Golden Gate International Exposition.

Ferries to Sausalito depart from the north side dock of the **Ferry Building**, an Embarcadero landmark for many years.

Nob and Russian Hills are more easily reached by cable car from downtown San Francisco than on foot. Either way, Nob Hill is reached via Powell, California and Mason Sts. It was given its name (short for nabob) after the 1870s when the 'Big Four' railroad tycoons and the Comstock Lode 'Silver Kings' built palatial homes here.

Leland Stanford's mansion (where the Stanford Court Hotel now stands) was the first 'Big Four' grand house. The Mark Hopkins Hotel is sited where railroad baron Mark Hopkins built a place, and the Fairmont Hotel was where 'Silver King' James Fair decided on a notable residence.

At the corner of California and Mason Sts, the **Pacific Union Club** (one of the city's oldest and most exclusive clubs) was the home of 'Silver King' James Flood. Walk west on California St and you'll

Transamerica Building, San Francisco

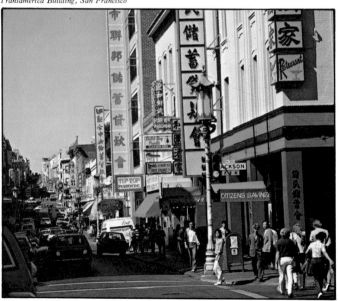

Grant Street, Chinatown, San Francisco

Square Rigger, Balclutha, *Fisherman's Wharf*

Cable Car in Union Square, San Francisco

come to **Huntington Park**. Continue on and you'll see **Grace Cathedral** on the site once occupied by the Charles Crocker mansion, another 'Big Four' masterpiece. The cathedral is one of the largest and loveliest of San Francisco's churches.

To get to Russian Hill from Nob Hill, take the northbound Hyde St cable car at the corner of California and Powell Sts, and get off at Lombard and Hyde. No-

thing is left here of historic note, but the views are superb and the atmosphere charming. It still attracts the arty folk as it always has done. The key street for tourists is **Lombard** which twists so much on its way down to Leavenworth (eight switchback curves), it's been termed 'the crookedest street in the world'. Very picturesque, but very difficult to maneuver its 90° angles with a car.

Lombard, 'crookedest street in the world'

One block north on Leavenworth and almost a block to the east on Chestnut is the **San Francisco Art Institute** whose lobby has changing exhibits and whose auditorium features a large Diego Rivera mural. Four blocks south on Leavenworth and a half block east on Green St, you'll see an octagonal house. Although a private residence, this architectural style was at one time highly favored in the Russian Hill area. Continue to the end of Green St for a view of Telegraph Hill and the East bay.

Another delightful street is **Macondray Lane** accessible via Jones and

Green Sts, downhill. Follow the Lane east to Taylor St, then head south to Vallejo St and east through **Coolbrith Park**, named after a Californian poetess.
Golden Gate Park is a very extensive park that requires a lot of time for full exploration. The entrance is at Stanyan and Fell Sts, where the Park Lodge has information on current exhibits and activities.

To the north of the main drive known as J.F. Kennedy Drive, the **Conservatory** open daily from 0800–1620, was modelled after Kew Gardens. Tropical plants from around the globe are on permanent dis-

Conservatory, Golden Gate Park, San Francisco

play here while seasonal flowers are to be viewed in the west wing's exhibition room. To the south by the main drive is the **John McLaren Rhododendron Dell** where 20 acres of magnificent rhododendrons form the dell named for the Scottish landscape gardener who created much of the park, and who also was known to San Franciscans as 'Uncle John'.

Don't miss the **M.H. De Young Memorial Museum** (see Museums) and afterwards, take the short walk to the **Japanese Tea Garden**, a five-acre Oriental garden with miniature trees, Shinto shrines, and a wishing bridge – at its best in spring when the cherry blossoms are

Japanese Garden, Golden Gate Park

San Francisco, view from Twin Peaks

out. The **Music Concourse**, like the tea garden, was created for an 1894 exhibition. The outdoor auditorium seats thousands and when the weather's good, band concerts are given here on Sundays and holidays.

To the south is the **California Academy of Sciences** (see Museums) and to the west of it, **Shakespeare's Garden of Flowers**. If there's a tree, plant, or flower mentioned in a Shakespearian epic, it's here. On South Drive is the **Strybing Arboretum and Botanical Gardens**, a highlight for botanists. A good number of the 5,000 plus plants growing here are unique. Native California plants have their own section and in the James Noble Conifer Collection, almost 400 species of conifers grow. In the Garden of Fragrance, plants that are pleasant to smell or to touch, are included and their labels are printed in braille.

Off South Drive to the right is **Stowe Lake**, the park's central reservoir for irrigation and a popular spot for boating. Golden Gate Park boasts many artificial lakes, but this is the biggest and most kinds of small boats may be rented here. It surrounds **Strawberry Hill** which you walk to via stepping stones across the lake. A path spirals to the top – 412ft (126m) for a panoramic vista.

West on the main drive, you'll pass **Prayer Book Cross** which commemorates the first use of the Book of Common Prayer on the West Coast by Sir Francis Drake's chaplain. Take Cross Over Drive and you'll come to **Lloyd Lake** and **Portals of the Past** where several marble columns stand. They are all that remained of A.N. Towne's Nob Hill mansion after the 1906 fire.

You may not expect to find buffalo in San Francisco, but if you continue on the main drive, that's precisely what you'll find in the **Buffalo Paddock**. At the park's western limits is a 47-ton sloop, **Amundsen's Ship Gjoa**. This Norwegian-built ship was the first to sail through the Northwest Passage and was a sealer before being bought by Amundsen, the Arctic explorer.

The 49 Mile Scenic Drive

This is clearly marked with the name and by a white seagull head on a blue background and leads to Mission Dolores. Start at Bay St and follow the signs west through the Marina District. You'll pass the **Palace of Fine Arts** (see Museums) and come to the **Presidio**, the entrance is at Lombard and Lyon Sts, where a detailed map is available. Today it is an army headquarters. (Presidios were the military attachment to the early missions.) Presidio troops figured in the Civil War, the Spanish-American War, the Philippine Insurrection, the Mexican border troubles, both World Wars, the Korean War and the Vietnam War. The main historic site in the Presidio today is the Army Museum, San Francisco's oldest adobe building. This is the start of a two-mile (3km) ecology trail – 80,000 trees planted since the 1880s on the once bare sand hills and rocks.

Follow the route and you'll pass the **California Palace of the Legion of Honor** (see Museums) in Lincoln Park on your way to **Cliff House** and **Seal Rocks**. From the Cliff House restaurant and bar you can see and hear a noisy bunch of sea lions playing offshore 400ft (120m) below. Some can always be seen whatever time of year, though the majority leave in June/July for Ano Nuevo Island to breed. A short uphill walk from Cliff House brings you to **Sutro Heights**, once the home of the man who broke the 'Silver Kings' monopoly – Adolph Sutro. The house has gone but his park remains.

Travel south on Great Highway and you'll see the beaches: Ocean Beach to the west, popular in warm weather but dangerous for swimming. Playland at the Beach to the east of the highway is a rowdy amusement park. On Sloat Blvd, at 46th Ave is the **San Francisco Zoo**, open 1000–1700. All the animals are displayed in realistically designed habitats in 70 acres of grounds. Next door is a children's playground and in the area is **Fleishhacker Pool**, an outdoor salt water pool

San Francisco City Hall

1000ft (300m) long by 150ft (32m) wide. From April to November it's open 0900–1700.

Still following the 49-Mile Drive, you'll pass through Golden Gate Park and on to the top of **Twin Peaks**, for a splendid view. Both the Indians and Spanish created legends around these two mountains, the one 910ft (277m) and the other 903ft (275m). (San Francisco's highest hill is Mount Davidson, 938ft (286m), which is about 5mi (8km) south on Portola Dr, but you may only walk up Mt Davidson.)

Eventually at 16th and Dolores Sts is **Mission Dolores** (see Missions). The Drive continues west to the Bay and on into the downtown area where you can visit the Civic Center.

San Francisco Civic Center comprises the City Hall (at Van Ness Ave, Polk, McAllister and Grove Sts) which has gold decorated domes and is a particularly impressive building, rising as it does 308ft (93m). It was partially designed by Arthur Brown Jr, as was the Civic Auditorium on Grove St with a 10,000 seating capacity and room for 2,400 more in adjacent halls. The State Building is at McAllister, Polk and Larkin Sts, and the public library's main branch is at Larkin, Fulton, McAllister and Hyde Sts.

Across from City Hall stands the **War Memorial Opera House** and the Veterans' Auditorium Building whose top floor is the **San Francisco Museum of Art**. (See Museums.)

If you must see **Haight-Ashbury** (there's not really anything to see but people), take Van Ness to Market, to Haight and go north. To reach the **Japanese Cultural and Trade Center**, take Geary Blvd to Laguna. This is the focal point of 'Japantown' which stretches to the north. Features include a kabuki theater restaurant, shops that sell anything and everything from Japan, unusual grocery stores and Japanese restaurants. Traditional celebrations like the Cherry Blossom Festival are also held here.

The Bridges

No one can talk about San Francisco without mention of its bridges, of which the Golden Gate is undoubtedly the most famous. A circular tour of the three main Bay Area ones can be made by car. A loop that covers the San Francisco-Oakland Bay Bridge, the Richmond-San Rafael Bridge and the Golden Gate will be about 50mi (80km). **The San Francisco-Oakland Bay Bridge** is one of the world's longest bridges – 4¼mi (7km). It was opened in 1936 and cost $77,200,000. Between the city and Yerba Buena Island, it is a suspension span, and from the island to Oakland, cantilever. **Richmond-San Rafael Bridge** runs over water for just over four miles (6km). It connects the Marin and Contra Costa shores.

One of the favourite photography locations is at Vista Point on the northern approach to **Golden Gate Bridge**. There's an eye-level view of the suspension cables and a grand view to the east and south. Off to the west are the Needles offshore rocks, Horseshoe Bay, and Fort Baker. Most of the credit for the Golden Gate Bridge is due to its engineer, Joseph Strauss. Up until 1964, it was the world's longest single-span suspension bridge. It opened in 1937, is 1.7mi (2.7km) long and cost $35,000,000.

San Francisco–Oakland Bay Bridge

Golden Gate Bridge

Alameda   F5
An island city in San Francisco Bay,
sharing Oakland's harbor. Formerly, it
was an important aviation center while
today it is a naval air station. Plenty of
beaches and good boating in the seven
marinas and yacht harbors are the main
visitor attractions. There are several municipal golf courses, parks and accommodations include a TraveLodge.

Alcatraz   F5
The infamous 'prison' island in San Francisco Bay, now on sightseeing tour itineraries. Since 1858 it has been a fortification,
a US military prison, an army disciplinary
barracks, a federal penitentiary and an
American Indian stronghold.

Last of the Rock's inmates left in 1963
but for the 18 months prior to 1971, it was
occupied by Indians protesting about US
government treatment of the native
Americans. The National Park Service
opened it to the public in October 1973
running two-hour conducted tours from
the San Francisco waterfront, 1¼mi (2km)
away. Although many of its buildings
were gutted by Indian fires or razed when
the Rock's future was unknown, the main
prison block can still be seen, with its steel
bars, claustrophobic cells, mess hall, library, and 'dark holes'. The exercise yard
with its concrete bleachers and towering
walls topped by guard towers and cat-
walks also remains.

Three former inmates did actually
make an escape from Alcatraz in 1962 by
tunneling out with sharpened spoons!
This feat took years to accomplish but
they were never traced.

Auburn   B9
In 1848 this was a mining camp known as
North Fork Dry Diggins which was later
renamed for Auburn in New York. The
old part of town – along Lincoln Way,
Sacramento, Commercial and Court Sts –
has all been restored. A collection of old
mining equipment plus Indian artifacts
are displayed at the **Placer County
Museum** on High St open 1000–1600
Mon.–Fri., to 1700 on weekends.

Fulsom Lake State Recreation Area
provides sporting activities like riding,
boating, fishing, swimming, and waterskiing. Camping is available in the park and
motels in town include Best Western.
Auburn holds a Placer County Fair in July
and a Gold Country Fair in September.

Big Sur   M6
An area of great scenic dramatic beauty
about 30mi (48km) south of Monterey on
State 1, between the Santa Lucia range
and the Pacific. Accommodations include
the Ventana and Big Sur Lodge and the
key tourist area is **Pfeiffer-Big Sur** State
Park which has its own lodge and campsites. Fishing, swimming, and naturalist
programs are among what's offered.

Alcatraz

Big Sur

Calistoga C4

It was a Mormon, Sam Brannan, who recognized that the natural qualities of hot water geysers and mineral springs, in 1859, would make this area a superb spa. He renamed it in honor of both the state and New York's Saratoga. Today, many vines are cultivated in its environs, as can be seen on a tour of Sterling Vineyards. Old Faithful Geyser of California on Tubbs Lane is a 60ft (18m) high geyser that erupts regularly.

Other natural attractions include the nearby **Petrified Forest** five miles (8km) to the west which contains redwood trees millions of years old, and **Mt St Helena**, eight miles (13km) north is the area where Robert Louis Stevenson honeymooned and wrote *The Silverado Squatters*. A park named for him is located on top of Mt St Helena (this is not the volcano which erupted in April 1980; that is Mt St Helens, in Washington State).

Carmel   K6

Sister city (although it's little more than a village) to Monterey on the Monterey Peninsula, set on a curve of beach. It was named by the Spanish in honor of the Carmelite friars and is a beauty spot adopted by many artists. There are no skyscrapers or giant hotels but good accommodations include Carmel Sands, Tradewinds Inn and Horizon Inn. Restaurants tend to be intimate and atmospheric. L'Escargot and la Marmite are both recommended French ones. Carmel also has some theater restaurants plus its own small regular theater. A Bach festival takes place here in July.

The Barnyard is *the* shopping area in Carmel making good use of rustic barns although there are plenty of other boutique and gallery complexes. Carmel's Mission (see below) was Serra's burial place.

A few miles along the coast from Carmel is the **Point Lobos** State Reserve. Its name, taken from the Spanish, means sea wolves (sea lions) and they can be seen on the rocks and in the surf. Point Lobos is also unique for its vegetation – wild mint covers the southern headland while the Monterey Cypress still grows wild in these parts.

San Carlos Borromeo Mission, Carmel

Fresno   K13

A bustling city located in the center of the state in the heart of the San Joaquin Valley. It was founded when the population of Millerton moved to the railroad line. Today Fresno claims to be the largest agricultural producer in the US, handling more than $1 million worth of fruit daily.

Visit **Roeding Park** which is famous for its variety of trees and shrubs, from arctic to tropical, covering 157 acres. Located on West Belmont Ave and Route 99, the park's other features include rose and camellia gardens, a playland and zoo.

Forestiere Underground Gardens on West Shaw Ave are five acres worth of rooms, gardens and grottoes. there are science exhibits on view at the **Discovery Center** on North Winery Ave, with summer evening telescope viewing from dusk to 2200. Places of natural beauty include **Millerton Lake** State Recreation Area, 21mi (34km) northeast. In this 6000 plus acreage, there are opportunities for swimming, fishing, boating, hiking, riding, and camping. Many of the state's famous national parks like the **Sierra National Forest**, are within easy access. Accommodations are plentiful, including Best Westerns, TraveLodges, a Hyatt, Hilton and Holiday Inn. Fresno has an April rodeo and an October fair.

Healdsburg   C3

A good base for canoeing – on the American, Russian, and Sacramento Rivers from April to October, and year round on the Colorado River. It's also in the heart of wine country – Russian River Wine Rd alone has 20 wineries. Tasting tours are also available at turn-of-the-century Simi on Healdsburg Ave, and Souverain Cellars five miles (8km) north.

Lake Tahoe   A12

A particularly clear blue lake that spreads its way into two states: California and Nevada. John Fremont discovered it in 1844 on his way to California from Oregon. Mark Twain camped on its shores and wrote that its colour was 'lapis lazuli set in a ring of emerald'.

Today, the whole area is highly developed. It is one of the country's highest lakes – 6200ft (1890m) above sea level and is 23mi (37km) long. Bases are **King's Beach** on the Californian side; **Tahoe Vista** at the northern end; **Tahoe City** and **Tahoma** on the western shore; **South Lake Tahoe** at the southern tip.

Lodi   E8

The northernmost town in the San Joaquin Valley, surrounded by vineyards. Lodi is especially known to be home of the Tokay grape. A tour of the Guild wineries and distilleries is one of those worth taking. Every September Lodi holds a Grape Festival and National Wine Show on its Festival Grounds, a celebration that includes a flower show, grape displays, and entertainment.

Visit **Lodi Lake Park** and **Zoo** five miles (8km) south which boasts a public swimming pool, Japanese, rose, and camellia gardens and a history museum. Camanche South Shore, 24mi (38km) east has several watersport facilities, fishing, boating, riding, tennis, and campsites.

Mammoth Lakes G16

Thirty lakes lie in a 9000ft (2740m) basin at Mammoth Mountains, but five of them are tourist destinations: Lake Mary, Lake Mamie, Twin Lakes, Lake George, and Horseshoe Lake. In summer, take the gondola ride up Mammoth Mountain or go on a guided pack and saddle trip. In winter, there is good skiing on challenging slopes. There are many mountain lodges in the area.

Situated about 30mi (48km) south of Yosemite National Park on US 395.

Modesto G9

A processing, shipping, and marketing center named for a San Francisco banker who was too modest to publicize his own name. It is a gateway to Yosemite on State 99 and the key to the area's prosperity is nearby Don Pedro Dam. See the **McHenry Museum** which has historical exhibits in period rooms and the children's park on South Morton Blvd, in Beard Brook Park. Also the Miller Horse and Buggy Ranch on Yosemite Blvd, 10mi (16km) east whose features include 19th-century firefighting equipment, delivery and Wells Fargo wagons and stagecoaches plus wooden-frame bicycles.

Turlock Lake State Recreation Area 23mi (37km) east offers swimming, fishing, boating, and campgrounds, while the **Don Pedro Lake** Recreational Area, 37mi (60km) east is composed of the 26mi (41km) long lake formed by the Dam. Swimming, boating and trout fishing here, too. Modesto motels include Holiday Inn, Best Western, and TraveLodge.

Monterey K6

A delightful port on a scenic peninsula, first sighted by Cabrillo but named by Vizcaino in 1602 for the Spanish Count Monte-Ray. It was rediscovered by Junipero Serra's missionary expedition who founded the presidio here and the Mission San Carlos de Borromeo at Carmel (a sister city).

Monterey became the capital of California as the Spanish knew it but in 1822

Monterey Harbor

under the Mexican regime, it alternated with Los Angeles as a provincial capital. It was in Monterey that the first legislature met and drew up California's first constitution. The American flag was raised here when the town was captured in 1849.

For a long time, Monterey was a whaler's retreat but once the fishing industry had expanded, it became a terminus for the anchovy and sardine fleets. The canneries and the people who lived around them prompted John Steinbeck to write *Cannery Row* and *Sweet Thursday*.

These days, Monterey is a quiet place famous for its seafood restaurants. Try any of them along Cannery Row, like York, a well-established dining spot. A block above Cannery Row, the Sardine Factory is also good. Gallatin's is set in a restored 1840 adobe house.

There are many motels in the area. Among the recommended are Cypress Gardens and Del Monte Pines. One of the best hotels is Del Monte's Hyatt House at Fisherman's Wharf which has a number of sporting facilities including riding, golf, fishing and tennis, plus therapy pools and sauna.

Entertainment is not of the jazzy type although there is a jazz festival held in Monterey in September and a theater in town. Golf is the top sport on the peninsula – played at Del Monte's 18-hole course, the Laguna Seca Golf Ranch or at famous private Pebble Beach. Fishing is another sport much indulged in, especially for salmon. (The Monterey Salmon Derby lasts from May until September.) Fishing and boating arrangements may be made at Fisherman's Wharf.

Colton Hall, Monterey

See **Monterey State Historic Park** on Olivier St, where a number of old houses are open most of the year from 0930–1630. Among them: Robert Louis Stevenson's house, now a museum, but the writer's temporary home in 1879 when he said this was 'the greatest meeting place of land and water in the world'. Larkin House on Calle Principal was a consulate from 1843–6 during the time that Thomas Larkin was US consul to Mexico in Monterey (the first and only one). Casa del Oro on Scott and Oliver Sts is a restored general store. Pacific House (1847) contains Indian relics. The Custom House is the state's oldest government building, built in 1827 and located at Fisherman's Wharf. And the First Theater was built adobe style as a boarding house and saloon.

Monterey's **Presidio** at Pacific St dates from 1770 and has several sites of interest plus a museum with historic regional artifacts and dioramas. Open Thurs.–Mon. 0900–1230 and 1330–1600. The **Royal Presidio Chapel** of San Carlos de Borromeo on Church St has one of the most fancy facades of any Mission.

California's first constitution was written in **Colton Hall Museum** when it was a town hall. Open 1000–1200 and 1300–1700.

The biggest attraction in Monterey is the **17-Mile Drive** which will take you around the peninsula from Pacific Grove to Carmel's Mission and back to Monterey. Scenically, this is a particularly beautiful route passing Seal Rock, Cypress Point, Spyglass Hill, and Pebble Beach golf courses along the way.

On 17-Mile Drive, Monterey

Napa Valley/ Sonoma County   C3

California's wine country – an easy drive from San Francisco along US 101, then State Highways 37, 121, and 12. There are many major wineries in the region, most of which are open to the general public for touring and sampling. Among them are: Beringer in St Helena; Christian Bros at Mont LaSalle and Sterling just south of Calistoga.

The **Bothe-Napa Valley** State Park is a delightful area for picnicking and hiking or swimming. A few miles further on, Calistoga is a health spa. While in the county, also see the Napa County Historical Society Museum.

Oakland   F5

Oakland's Municipal Center is at the south end of Lake Merritt, said to be the world's largest natural body of salt water contained within one city. There are 160 acres of it providing an excellent boating mecca, but also a national duck refuge. At the northern end of the lake, a children's playground puts nursery rhymes into animated settings and features rides like the Oakland Acorn Express miniature train and a miniature replica of a Mississippi River steamboat.

The waterfront area known as **Jack London Square** is entertaining and colourful and one of the best places to eat. First and Last Chance Saloon here was built from timber taken from old whalers. Before it became a seamen's hangout, it was used as a bunkhouse for oyster-bed workmen. These days, although the setting is historical (with Jack London photographs and letters around the place) be prepared for anything!

Eccentric California poet, Joaquin Miller (Poet of the Sierras) lived in an estate that reflected himself – evident when you look at his preserved home at Mountain Blvd. The house called 'The Abbey' was built in 1866 and is surrounded by pleasantly wooded grounds. It was from a point in what is now the Joaquin Miller Park that John Charles Frémont, the explorer, first saw and named the Golden Gate.

Petaluma   D4

A poultry centre, as its nickname 'World's Egg Basket' implies. But in this area visitors come to see the **Casa Grande** of General Mariano Vallejo, the Mexican commandant general of Northern California, which was supposed to be the largest Spanish ranch house in Northern California and was the headquarters of Vallejo's 75,000 acre Rancho Petaluma, today a state historical monument.

Sacramento   C8

The state capital of California, reached via the San Francisco-Oakland Bridge and Interstate 80 and 85mi (136km) northeast. The State Capitol and capitol park are located between 9th and 15th Sts. The park comprising 40 landscaped acres encircles the **Capitol** which was built in 1874. The latter's dome is 275ft (84m) high and gold leafed. Inside the building are the legislative chambers, statuary and murals. Open daily from 0700–2100.

The adobe house built in 1839 by Swiss entrepreneur, Johan Sutter, in its restored form, can be seen on L St. **Sutter's Fort** today is a park and museum housing stage coaches, gold from Sutter's Mill, and in the **State Indian Museum** aspects of the Indian dugout canoes, and Indian burial grounds way of life, and death. Open daily 1000–1700.

Art treasures are on display at the **Crocker Art Gallery** on O St. There are, in addition to the permanent collection, changing exhibits of sculptures, paintings, prints, bronzes, and tapestries.

The **Governor's Mansion** on 16th and H Sts is designated a historical landmark and is open daily 1000–1700. The **Pony Express Building** at Second and J Sts was originally constructed as a post office in 1853 and only later became a pony express terminus. The Embarcadero next to it has become **Old Sacramento** – the city as it was between 1849 and 1870.

The railroad station at Fifth and I Sts houses a number of murals relating to the first trans-continental railroad. The famous Huntington Locomotive (1863) stands in front of it.

San Jose   H6

The first state capital (1849–51) and today an important missile and electronics center. See the municipal rose garden on Naglee and Dana where 5000 of the flowers have been arranged in a formal garden. Also on Naglee, the **Egyptian Temple** and **Oriental Museum of Rosicrucians** has a good collection of Egyptian and oriental antiquities.

Alum Rock Park (a 700-acre municipal park) is often called 'Little Yosemite' because of its natural formations, but it was named for a 200ft (61m) cliff whose surface is coated with alum dust. Mineral springs in rocky grottoes dot the area. As an added attraction, there are canyon trails, an aviary, and a deer park.

San Rafael   E4

One of the residential communities of Marin County, across the Golden Gate Bridge, and the county seat. It was developed around an early mission (Mission

San Rafael Arcángel) and is today a trading and industrial center. Take a look at **Marin County Civic Center**, a complex designed by Frank Lloyd Wright – and one of his last major projects.

San Simeon O8

The 'fantasy' estate of William Randolph Hearst, born into a wealthy San Franciscan family in 1863. He was given the *Examiner* when only 24 and between his own efforts and dad's money, made it into the West Coast's most powerful paper.

San Simeon sits atop a knoll overlooking the Pacific, along the great scenic route between Los Angeles and San Francisco. Hearst called the hill La Cuesta Encantada (The Enchanted Hill) and at one time the ranch occupied 340,000 acres. He began building his 'castle' in 1919, gathering objets d'art from around the world. Building continued until Hearst's death in 1951 and was never finally completed to his specifications.

The castle itself resembles a medieval fortress with a refectory, a high-ceilinged noble room where there are hand carved life-size statues of saints and 16th-century silk banners; the assembly room with priceless tapestries and marble medallions, each weighing a ton. There is an indoor gold-inlaid Roman pool, gardens, pools, and statuary all over. Altogether, the collections are valued at $50 million. San Simeon is administered by the State of California and is so large, there are several separate tours of it available.

Santa Cruz J6

A noted resort city and fishing centre. You can fish off the municipal pier; surf, swim, or deep sea fish in the ocean. A wide beach suits the sunbathers and along the boardwalk is an amusement park and casino. Restaurants, gift shops and boating concessions line the half-mile pier. **Mission Santa Cruz** is only a half-size reproduction of the original.

Santa Rosa D4

The seat of Sonoma County. Luther Burbank chose this region in 1875 as the site for an experimental farm. That 1½-acre piece of land is now known as **Burbank Memorial Gardens** at Santa Rosa Ave and Tupper St. The Burbank home and most of his plant discoveries are to be seen here, as is the horticulturist's grave.

Another point of interest is the **First Baptist Church** on B St between 5th and 6th Sts in Juilliard Park, which was built in 1873 from the wood of one redwood tree.

Sausalito F4

A seaside community across San Francisco's bay reached by bridge or ferry. It has a riviera atmosphere helped by the mass of flowers and the houses which cling to the hillside. There are plenty of discotheques, chic boutiques, bars, and restaurants along the colorful waterfront. Sally Stanford's Valhalla was founded by a famous San Francisco madam.

Swimming pool, Hearst Castle, San Simeon

Sonoma D4

One of California's most historic towns with clear directions to the major sights. In one corner of the town plaza is the spot where California was proclaimed a republic and the Bear Flag was raised.

In the vicinity of the **Mission San Francisco Solano de Sonoma** (see Missions), a number of buildings date from the time when Mariano Vallejo was commandant general of Northern California. You can see the soldiers' barracks (1836); the adobe Blue Wing Tavern whose balcony is supported by hand-hewn redwood posts (1840).

Vallejo laid out the town of Sonoma. His home, **Lachryma Montis** (Tear of the Mountain), is located to the north of Third St West and was named for the nearby natural spring. The house built in 1851 was the most luxurious in the area at the time and is now a state historical monument. Timbers and brick for this Victorian-style residence were brought round the Horn from Europe. Vallejo's grave, marked by a black granite monument, is in the Sonoma Cemetery.

A couple of miles from the plaza are the **Buena Vista Vineyards** which date from 1832 when the Hungarian colonel, Agoston Haraszthy, planted some of California's first grapes. The original cellars were destroyed by the 1906 earthquake but have since been restored. The winery still operates and samples are available. Open daily 1000–1700.

Sonora F11

A colorful town stretching across seven hills and seat of Tuolumne County. It was named by Mexican miners for their home state and has seen turbulent times. The Big Bonanza, the richest pocket mine in the Mother Lode was brought in here – $160,000 of almost pure gold – in one day. Sonora was also the setting for several Mark Twain stories.

Columbia State Historic Park, four miles (6km) to the north is where the gold town of Columbia has been restored. **Moaning Caverns**, 12mi (19km) north on Moaning Cave Road, have some interesting formations to be viewed from a 100ft (30m) spiral staircase. Guided tours may also be taken of the **Mercer Caverns** discovered in 1885, ten miles (16km) away. To the northeast and southeast of town is the **Stanislaus National Forest** which contains the **Emigrant Wilderness** and part of the **Mokelumne Wilderness**. There are recreational areas for summer watersports and wintersports.

Three Rivers L16

A peaceful place in a lovely shaded valley along the Kaweah River. The region offers fine fishing, hiking, and swimming. At Lake Kaweah, two miles (3km) west, there is a marina and opportunities to waterski. Three Rivers is the gateway to **Sequoia** and **Kings Canyon National Parks** (see Parks) whose entrance is two miles (3km) from town.

Columbia, Sonora

LAS VEGAS

History Fur traders and trappers were venturing into Nevada in the 1820s, but it was the Mormons who were the state's first permanent settlers. In the 1850s, some 30 Mormons arrived in this valley, picking the location to help protect a Salt Lake City-Los Angeles mail route. They called their settlement Bringhurst, built an adobe fort and started to cultivate some of the meadowland, not an easy thing in such a remote desert location. They established a lode mine operation at Potosi Mountain, 30mi (48km) to the south but they didn't recognize the value of their find – that the lead had such a high silver content.

Failing to make a success of the settlement, the Mormons returned to Utah in 1857 and Las Vegas (a name which means 'The Meadows' in Spanish) was left to the Indians and the elements. It was 're-discovered' in 1865 by a former gold miner who obtained title to much of the land around the springs along with the water rights. Octavius Gass and his partners started a ranching and farming community which continued into the 20th century.

In fact, at this time, Las Vegas was part of Arizona, not Nevada at all. It was not until 1866 that the part of Arizona north of the Colorado River plus a 60-mile stretch of Utah, was ceded to Nevada.

As with so many cities out West, it was the railroad which was the turning point in Las Vegas' growth. Just after the turn of the century, it became a major diversion point in the San Pedro, Los Angeles, and Salt Lake Railroad. In 1902 the railroad bought land and water rights and in 1905 (when it had become the Union Pacific), it sold off 1,200 lots in one day, for $265,000. The 'town' then was little more than a few ranches and tented structures alongside the tracks.

In keeping with the West's image, gambling parlors and saloons soon sprang up and other businesses followed them. By 1909, 800 people were living in Las Vegas, five of whom were lawyers, three doctors, two dentists, one a plumber, and 11 saloon keepers. It was incorporated as a city in 1911.

An important year for Las Vegas was 1928 when Congress passed the Boulder Canyon Project Act enabling the Hoover Dam to be built on the Colorado River. The site chosen was a desolate spot 25mi (40km) south of the community and construction began in 1931. Close to $50 million was appropriated for the project, the most ambitious to that time.

Thousands poured into Las Vegas and neighboring Boulder City to work on the project.

Oddly enough, it was the same year that the state legislature passed a law legalizing gambling and until recently, Nevada has been the only American state to boast legal gambling. At about the same time, the residency requirement for divorce became law and soon Las Vegas (and Reno) became the best destinations for a quickie divorce. Six weeks and hey presto!

In 1935, the new dam was dedicated by Franklin D. Roosevelt as Boulder Dam (it was renamed Hoover Dam only after World War II). It became a major tourist attraction, but it was due to a group of Los Angeles investors that Las Vegas took its first steps towards becoming a resort capital. In 1940, they purchased land on US 91 and built the El Rancho Vegas hotel. The hotel (now demolished) was the cornerstone of what is now the celebrated 'Strip'.

Around this time, too, the US government, recognizing the expanse of land available, and the good weather conditions, built a military air training base. Then called Las Vegas Army Airfield, it is now Nellis AFB. Meanwhile, the 'Strip' was growing. The Last Frontier was erected as was Bugsy Siegel's Fabulous Flamingo. More and more entertainment and gambling palaces mushroomed and during this colourful era, Las Vegas earned its reputation as the 'town with no clocks'.

Accommodations There really is a wide variety of hotels and motels, both along the three mile 'Strip' (Las Vegas Blvd South) and in the downtown area, sometimes caustically referred to as 'Glitter Gulch'. Competition is so fierce that rates aren't half as bad as one might think and one thing all the major establishments have in common is gambling. Since sports

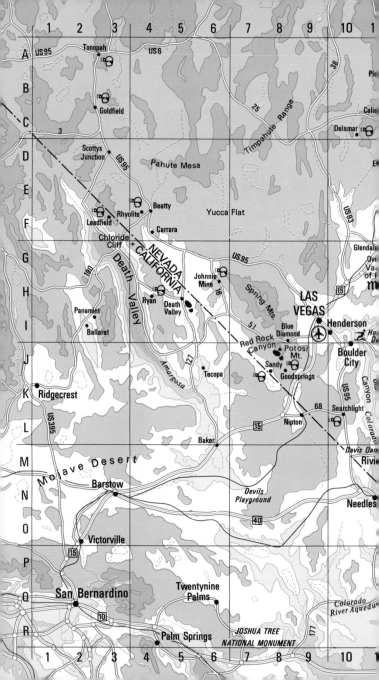

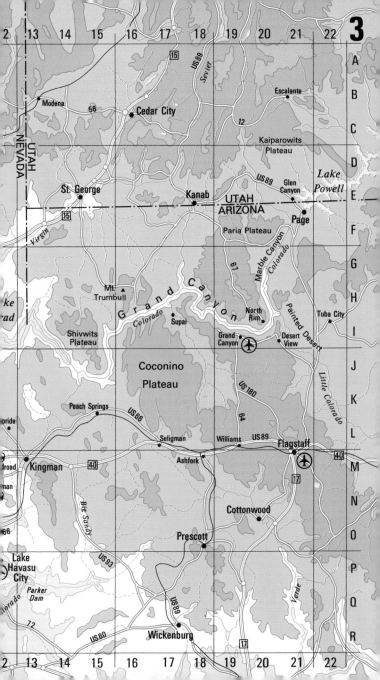

are another Las Vegas 'thing', top properties feature a variety of amenities from tennis courts to health clubs.

Top on the strip is Caesar's Palace, a film set place you don't ever have to leave. Famed for its big name entertainment, it's the ultimate in Las Vegas kitsch with enough statuary to make Rome wince and even basic rooms which are ornate. The Aladdin is for those who like a thousand and one nights atmosphere, and the Sahara is a little quieter and more elegant. Circus-Circus is a family-style carousel of a hotel with plenty to do for the children. There's an enormous Hilton, the MGM Grand and the Dunes. Union Plaza is a good downtown hotel near all the action and the Mint Hotel is another downtown favorite. The Golden Nugget Old West casino now has its own hotel. Motels, both just off the Strip and downtown, are plentiful and cost far less money of course than those familiar names above.

Eating Out Food is incredibly good value in Las Vegas, probably because gambling revenues help subsidize it. Quantities and quality, even in the nightclubs, are far superior to most other places. There are cheap diner breakfasts, all-you-can-eat buffets – and it's all available practically any hour of the day or night. Steaks and seafood are the prime offerings, but there's a smattering of ethnic restaurants as well.

Some of the best buffet bets are at the Holiday Casino on Las Vegas Blvd S, the Mint on Fremont St, and the champagne brunch at Caesar's. Good seafood can be found at the Lobster Trap on E. Sahara St and as its name suggests, the Golden Steer specializes in all kinds of steaks. What's more, this restaurant has been around for 17 years – and that's a long time in Las Vegas! One of the most plush places in town is considered to be the Palace Court but it's pricey.

Las Vegas

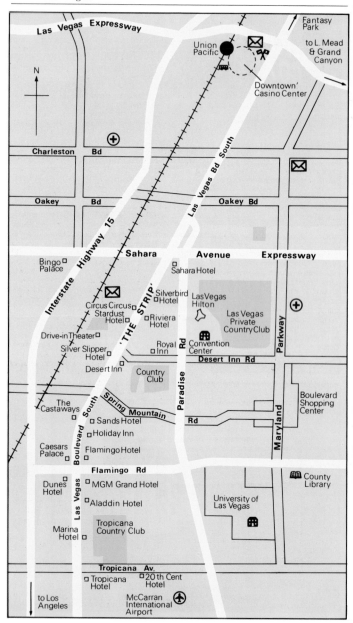

Entertainment Nightlife is what Las Vegas is all about which is why it can attract top entertainers every day of the year to its hotel lounges and to its big nightclub theaters. Many an overseas visitor will opt for one of the large flashy show productions, with showgirls, bands, super costuming, and everything else that looks like Broadway or Paris. The four which have been continuing for years are 'The Lido de Paris' at the Stardust; the 'Folies Bergere' at the Tropicana; the 'Casino de Paris' at the Dunes and 'Hallelujah Hollywood' at the MGM Grand. All lavish spectaculars.

Prices for such shows vary, as they may be sold as part of a nightclub tour, a cocktail show, and sometimes a dinner show. Entertainment in the hotel lounges, though, is usually free. All the top hotels have live lounge cabaret and many a performer who started off playing one of the Las Vegas resorts has ended up a superstar. You may see comics, singers, or musical groups playing anything from country 'n' western to rock.

Circus-Circus Hotel has a unique show with a continuous show of circus acts going on under a second storey big top right above all the casino action. The Union Plaza is also unique for Vegas, presenting Broadway-type musicals and plays. The Hacienda goes in for an ice extravaganza. One of the newer showplaces is the 7,500-seater theater for the performing arts at the Aladdin Hotel. The dome-shaped concert hall has hosted such top names as Earth, Wind and Fire.

Reservations must be made in advance for any show and unless it's part of an excursion, house guests do take priority at any of the hotels. As I mentioned, dinner is often included with the early show, but late shows are drinks only, and there's no cost at all for the circus. Headliner shows are obviously sold out first so if there's someone special, or some show you particularly wish to see, consider staying at the place where it's being presented. Otherwise, go early in the morning to make that night's reservation. Tipping – from the bellhop to the casino pit boss – does help!

There are non hotel clubs and discos, too, like the currently popular Victoria's on Decatur Blvd. The Silver Dollar Saloon features country 'n' western (E. Charlston Blvd) and The Royal Casino on Convention Center Dr is one of the better strip joints.

As for the gambling, there's every form of it, starting with slot machines which you'll reach before you reach a reception desk. They're hard to leave – the sound of jangling coins at the airport machines leaves you with a ring in your ears and maybe an empty pocket.

And then there's always marriage. It's as easy as saying 'I do' any day, any night. Las Vegas' wedding chapels are open 24 hours and will supply all you need for a quick service, including the bouquet. A license from the Las Vegas Marriage License Bureau is all that's required – no blood test, no waiting time. But remember what many another visitor to Las Vegas has found out that 'when you marry in haste, you're more than likely to repent at leisure' – which could mean the following morning with a hangover.

Sport Las Vegas is more than averagely sports minded and hosts many famous tournaments. One of the biggest in tennis is the Alan King Tennis Classic, held in April or May at Caesar's Palace, and nationally televised. A number of top boxing events are held in the town an an outgrowth of the more major events has been the appearance of many world-rated boxers in weekly fight cards. The Mint 400 Desert Race is an annual off-road race attraction, held every spring on the challenging desert terrain surrounding Vegas. The Showboat Invitational Bowling Tournament and its rich prize is another biggie to watch out for – held in January in the Showboat Hotel's 70-lane complex.

Not quite so big, but worthy of mention are the billiard, chess, trapshooting, horse riding, fishing, card game, wrist wrestling, and golfing events that are staged throughout the year. The University of Nevada's sports programme has made its own contribution and pros from all sports compete in the annual Dewar's Celebrity Pro Tourney at the Riviera Hotel.

The visitor doesn't have to be a voyeur – there are enough sports facilities for pleasure participants. The Strip's hotels alone provide 11 full-size golf courses and over 100 tennis courts. Just phone for a tee time or court reservation. Desert it may be, but watersports are equally available. In the Lake Mead National Recreational Area, there are nine marinas where fishing equipment, boats, and waterskis may be rented.

Excursions The number one excursion originating from Las Vegas is a scenic flight to the **Grand Canyon** (See Parks). Scenic Airlines, the pioneers of canyon air-ground tours, are today just one of several airlines offering this trip daily. Take-off is from McCarran International Airport and the narrated travel guide, via individual headphones, is available in several languages. On the way, you'll pass Hoover Dam and the upper reaches of Lake Mead, before spending 20 minutes below the canyon's upper rim.

Bright Angel Trail, Grand Canyon

Mather Point, Grand Canyon

From the South Rim, Grand Canyon

The scenic flight lands at Grand Canyon Airport, followed by lunch at the Canyon Squire Inn, and then to the observation point on the South Rim. Time is given for photography at several vantage points and to look through the shops and museum. A fixed price for this $7\frac{1}{2}$ hour package includes transport, food, and park fees. Also available ex-Las Vegas is a four-hour air-only tour and for a bird's eye view of Las Vegas itself, a one hour scenic flight is possible. Air tours of the Hoover Dam are another feature.

Daily chartered air-ground tours are also available to Disneyland (see Young West Coast) and to Death Valley (see Parks).

Only 20mi (32km) to the west of Las Vegas is a natural, and very different attraction – **Red Rock Canyon**. A round trip of the area will cover 60mi (97km) and there are several viewpoints along Red Rock Scenic Rd.

The canyon itself comprises 62,000 acres which show both usual and unusual forms of desert vegetation and wildlife. Wild burros and bighorn sheep move between the wind-sculpted sandstone formations and the recreation area has several camp and picnic sites. One of the most striking formations is **Red Rock Escarpment**, a 3,000ft (914m) formation of pinnacles and boulders, jutting from the canyon floor. To reach here, take West Charleston Blvd, from Interstate 15 for 16mi (25km) to the west where the scenic loop road begins. Before making the turn, continue on for $1\frac{1}{2}$mi ($2\frac{1}{2}$km) to Dedication Point where names and elevations of the varying points of interest are signposted in displays.

The loop trip is 13mi (20km). Stop two miles (3km) north of the turnoff at Calico Hills Vista – a magnificent panoramic view of red sandstone hills. Hikers can take a short marked trail to the bottom of a wooded ravine whose boulders the Paiute Indians called home 900 years ago.

One mile ($1\frac{1}{2}$km) further up the scenic road is Sandstone Quarry turnoff. Sandstone slabs in this area were used for Las Vegas homes many years ago. From here, hikers with stamina can climb to the east or north for a look at Indian petroglyphs and mescal pits in Brownstone Canyon. The quarry itself may be used for picnics.

Four and a half miles (7km) further on brings you to Willow Springs, another picnic site. (Nearest camping area is at La Madre Canyon, four miles (6km) northwest, but it is primitive.) For the next portion of the road, a real close-up of the multi-coloured escarpment is possible with three paved viewpoints giving

exceptional photo angles of the massive boulders, rock chimneys, and bluffs.

From West Charleston Blvd, heading south, you will reach a road leading to **Oak Creek Canyon** at the base of the escarpment. A trail to the north leads to **Pine Creek Canyon**, cool enough for maidenhair fern, columbine, and the stream orchid to grow. Throughout the canyon area, a number of plants and trees are in evidence: typical cacti and yuccas lower down; joshua trees and oaks; and ponderosa pines in the higher parts.

Back on the main road, about two miles (3km) from Oak Creek Rd, is **Spring Mountain Ranch** which is maintained by the Nevada Park System. This was once the retreat of Howard Hughes and before that, the residence of Vera Krupp, wife of the German munitions industrialist. Tours are available of the house with state rangers.

One of the key attractions of the park is **Bonnie Springs-Old Nevada**, a recreation of an old mining town of the 1800s when lawlessness was a way of life. Realistic shootings, lynchings, and bar room brawls illustrate the old days. Several stores line the main street as well as a theater and museum with a mine-shaft setting. The Bonnie Springs Ranch next door rents out horses. (Organized tours to this attraction are available from Las Vegas, to include a train ride in Old Nevada's park, admission to the wax museum, opera house and Dean Casper's house of miniature and animated woodcarvings – plus lunch and transport.)

Although this marks the southernmost boundary of the recreation area, two miles (3km) further south is **Blue Diamond**, a small community with a population of just over 200. It was once a favored stopping point for the '49ers and the Mormon pioneers who travelled the old Spanish trail from Santa Fe, New Mexico to Los Angeles, in the 1830s. Three miles further, the road intersects with the Blue Diamond Highway. Turn left and drive for 11mi (18km) to bring you back to Interstate 15.

Maps and information on the park may be obtained from the BLM, 4765 Vegas Dr, Las Vegas, Nevada 89108 (702 385 6403).

Interstate 15 equally leads to the **Valley of Fire**, some 50mi (80km) north of Las Vegas. Pre-historic Indians inhabited the place more than 20,000 years ago and later the valley was home to the Paiute tribes who have left us petroglyphs (pictures etched into the sandstone) to remember them by. The best area for these historic petroglyphs is **Atlatl Rock**, close to the park's centre. *Atlatl* is an Aztec word meaning 'spear launcher'. A legendary petroglyph area is *Mouse's Tank*, a hidden canyon. In this instance 'Mouse' is not the small creature the cat catches, but a renegade Indian whose small size and quick movements earned him the name. His 'tank' was a series of water potholes, suited for hiding out. 'Mouse' was finally apprehended by the law but his legend persists.

The **Lost City Museum** is located a few miles north of the park, in Overton. Archaeological relics and models of adobe style dwellings paint the picture of Indian life in the park, with preserved spear and arrow points, woven reed sandals and pottery on view.

Most unusual formation in the park is **Elephant Rock** so named because of its resemblance to that animal. There are many rocks bearing the same name, but this one has the most realistic resemblance. **Beehive Rocks** is also interesting for the weathered rocks give an impression of beehives.

Ghost towns proliferate in Nevada and offer the visitor a real glimpse of the Old West when mining might mean fame and fortune. Among those within easy access of Las Vegas, are: **Potosi** – on the old Spanish Trail, 25mi (40km) out of town and the state's oldest mine. Mine and tramway ruins can be explored here. **Goodsprings** – 35mi (56km) southwest of Las Vegas was a booming mining camp for lead and zinc at the turn of the century. Rocks, mine workings, and an abandoned railroad await the explorer. The Sandy Valley Area, 13mi (20km) west again, has a ghost town, **Sandy**, with a gold mill. **Eldorado Mountains**, 40mi (64km) south-west of Las Vegas are dotted with old mines. The Techatticup mine here produced over $2.5 million in gold prior to 1942. Between 1902 and 1909, **Searchlight**, 55mi (88km) south of the city, was a lively mining center, for a while rivalling Las Vegas itself. Tourists generally stop here on their way to Davis Dam and Cottonwood Cove on Lake Mohave. It is also the gateway to Christmas Tree Pass and Spirit Mountain.

More adventurous excursions may be made to Nye and Lincoln Counties where **Rhyolite** is one of the most famous old mining camps. Located 120mi (192km) away on State 58 off US 95, there are several building remains to intrigue tourists, including a railroad station which used to be termed the 'Dearborn St Station of the West'. In 1907, 10,000 people lived here. Now there are six. During the 1870s, **Pioche**, 193 mi (310km) northeast of Las Vegas was a rough and ready mining town, one that rivalled Tombstone for violence. Reached via US 93 it is now the county seat of Lincoln County.

One of the longest surviving mining developments was the **Johnnie Mine** on State Route 16, 13mi (20km) south from its junction with US 95. Prospectors were there as early as 1869, but it didn't become active until the 1900s and gold was found here as late as 1920.

Leadfield on the Titus Canyon Rd into Death Valley was a boom town of the 1920s and **Carrara**, 110mi (176km) northwest of Vegas thrived on marble quarrying after the First World War. But little remains of either. **Chloride Cliff**, 13mi (20km) west of Carrara, however, is a spectacular place to view Death Valley.

Former gold camp, **Delamar**, lies 160mi (258km) north of Vegas and still features interesting mill ruins and rock cabins. **Goldfield** and **Tonopah** were two more turn-of-the-century boom towns – 182mi (290km) and 206mi (332km) from the city. Some of the old mines still operate.

Venture into Arizona and you'll find more. **Goldroad** was where gold was first found in 1864 and **Mineral Park** has the ruins of stone and adobe buildings, while **Oatman** was active from 1900–1942. Ghost towns can be found around and in Death Valley (see Parks) but those closest to the Nevada border are Bodie, Panamint, Tecopa, Skidoo and Ryan.

Hoover Dam is more of a localized popular sightseeing excursion. It was created in the mid thirties to control flooding and generate electricity. By backing up the river to form the 115-mile-long (185km) Lake Mead, it has provided an enjoyable recreation area. The dam is 727ft (222m) high (or equivalent to 70 storeys) with a base that is 660ft (200m) thick. It took 4.4 million cubic yards (3.4 million cu m) of concrete to built it and it was the first archgravity dam to be built. At the time of its completion, it was claimed to be the 'eighth engineering wonder of the world'. It took five years to construct and the $175 million cost should be recovered in 1987.

Lake Mead is the largest man-made reservoir in the US with the ability to hold 31 million acre feet of water. It covers a surface area of 225mi (362km) with 500mi (200km) of shoreline and provides a year-round place for watersports. The huge Lake Mead National Recreational Area allows for fishing, boating, water skiing and, camping and includes Lake Mohave which is backed up by Davis Dam, 67mi (107km) south from Hoover.

The lake is one of the top bass fisheries and anglers can fish any time of year, day or night.

INDEX

All the main entries in the text are printed in heavy type. Where main entries have a map reference this is also printed in heavy type and is preceded by the page numbers of one of the three main maps. Where only page numbers appear in heavy type after an entry these refer to the maps of the Missions or the National Parks, or the plans of the four main cities.